The Sutter Family and the
Origins of Gold-Rush Sacramento

PORTRAIT OF JOHN A. SUTTER, JR., REPRODUCED
FROM A PAINTING PRESENTED TO SUTTER'S FORT
HISTORICAL MUSEUM BY MRS. ANNA SUTTER YOUNG

The Sutter Family and the Origins of Gold-Rush Sacramento

John A. Sutter, Jr.

Edited, with a biography by Allan R. Ottley
Introduction by Albert L. Hurtado

University of Oklahoma Press
Norman

Library of Congress Cataloging-in-Publication Data

Sutter, John Augustus, 1826–1897.
    [Statement regarding early California experiences]
    The Sutter family and the origins of Gold-Rush Sacramento /
John A. Sutter, Jr. ; edited, with a biography by Allan R. Ottley ;
introduction by Albert L. Hurtado.
        p.   cm.
    Originally published: Sacramento, Calif. : Sacramento Book
Collectors Club, 1943.
    Includes bibliographical references and index.
    ISBN 0-8061-3493-3 (pb. : alk. paper)
        1. Sutter, John Augustus, 1826–1897. 2. Pioneers—
California—Biography. 3. Gold miners—California—Biography.
4. Businessmen—California—Biography. 5. California—Gold
discoveries. 6. Frontier and pioneer life—California. 7. Frontier
and pioneer life—California—Sacramento. 8. Sacramento
(Calif.)—History—19th century. 9. Sacramento (Calif.)—
Biography. I. Ottley, Allan R. II. Title.

F865.S (Sutter)+
979.4'5404'092—dc21
[B]

                                                            2002067525

The paper in this book meets the guidelines for permanence and
durability of the Committee on Production Guidelines for Book
Longevity of the Council on Library Resources, Inc.

1   2   3   4   5   6   7   8   9   10

Thanks to Susan W. Travers and Judith Eitzen with the Sacramento Book Collectors Club for their assistance in making this publication possible. Originally published as publication no. 2 by the club under the title **Statement Regarding Early California Experiences.**

Contents

In a short time the whole history shall be exposed to
the public, under what circumstances and influences
my son has been persuaded by his advisers to consent
and agree to the propositions made to him.
It will astonish the world.

J. A. Sutter
—Sacramento Union, *Oct. 6, 1856*

Preface

JOHN A. SUTTER, JR., was the eldest son of the celebrated Captain Sutter of New Helvetia. He managed the Sutter property during most of the critical period between 1848 and 1851, and was himself the founder of the city of Sacramento. His *Statement Regarding Early California Experiences* is here printed for the first time.

By 1852 the great Sutter holdings in Sacramento had all been lost, and Sutter, Jr., penniless, ill, and despondent, had exiled himself in a wild part of the Mexican state of Sonora. He returned to California early in 1855, hoping to retrieve something of his lost fortune and anxious to justify or explain to his family and friends his part in losing it. It was at this time that he wrote the story of his life in California, telling how the property was lost and how he had been drugged and swindled. A few months after writing his apologia, Sutter, Jr., moved to Acapulco where he became a successful businessman and public official. He never returned to California.

His *Statement* is a straightforward and guileless account. It has the ring of truth about it, and its revelations are essential to a true understanding of the Sutter family and their part in the early history of Sacramento. Perhaps nowhere else is the unprincipled scramble for land in the Sacramento Valley so well portrayed. Although the manuscript has been consulted by some of the elder Sutter's biographers, its real importance has not been widely known. It is now published by the Sacramento Book Collectors Club in the belief that it will be a valuable addition to the printed sources for the history of early California. The manuscript, consisting of fifty-two carefully handwritten pages, is now in the collection of the California State Library. It was purchased by the

library in 1896 from Mr. N. E. White. How and where it was pre-
served from 1855 to 1896 is not known.

The details of Sutter, Jr.'s life are not familiar even to historians.
Almost nothing has been written about him, while perhaps too
many books about his more famous father have come off the
press. For that reason a short biography of him has been included
here as a companion piece to his *Statement.*

The *Statement* has been printed as it appears in the manuscript
with the exception of a few changes in style made to assist the
reader. Punctuation marks have been put in and omitted when
not to have done so would have perverted or confused the sense.
This, however, has been done sparingly, and no attempt at complete punctuation has been made. A few misspelled words which
might have caused the reader to stumble have been corrected in
square brackets; others have been left as they were. Several words
have been inserted in brackets to clarify the meaning. A few changes
in capitalization have been made, including the substitution of
San Francisco for Sutter's *Sanfrancisco.*

Many persons have contributed to the making of this book. Our
first debt of gratitude is to Miss Mabel R. Gillis, California State
Librarian, who generously granted permission to publish the manuscript. We also wish to thank the following: Miss Caroline Wenzel
of the State Library; Miss Grace Taylor, Miss Helen Mayden, Miss
Dorothy Drake, and others of the Sacramento City Library; Mrs.
Anna Sutter Young, only surviving child of Sutter, Jr., who granted
two interviews, wrote several letters, and loaned her collection of
her father's papers; Howard Joseph Sutter Hull, of Lancaster, Pennsylvania, who contributed many details on the life of his grandfather; P. M. Hamer, Chief, Division of Reference, the National
Archives, who supplied information on Sutter's official life in
Mexico; Mrs. E. J. Magnuson, of Minneapolis, who sent photostat
copies of several pages of Lienhard's manuscript *Memoiren*; Mr.
and Mrs. Amalio Gomez, of Sacramento, who assisted in the translation of several of the Sutter, Jr., Papers; Miss Concha J. Hudson,
of the American consular staff at Acapulco; and Carroll D. Hall,

Curator of Sutter's Fort, who enabled us to secure a copy of the portrait of Sutter, Jr., placed in the Fort by Mrs. Young.

George T. Smisor drove from Mexico City to Acapulco and generously spent considerable time digging out information about Sutter's activities there. As head of the printing department of the Sacramento Junior College, he has supervised the printing and designing of the book. His assistance has been invaluable.

Permission to quote copyrighted material was received from the following: Mrs. Marguerite E. Wilbur, for the use of quotations from *A Pioneer at Sutter's Fort, 1846-1850: the Adventures of Heinrich Lienhard*; Miss Dorothy H. Huggins, Secretary of the California Historical Society, for material from the Society's *Quarterly*; Mrs. Helen P. Van Sicklen, Secretary, and the directors of the Society of California Pioneers, for material from the *New Helvetia Diary*; the Oxford University Press, for quotations from James P. Zollinger's *Sutter, the Man and His Empire*; and Dr. Erwin G. Gudde, for permission to quote from *Sutter's Own Story*.

When publication was first planned by the club in 1941 the work was placed in the hands of a committee headed by Allan R. Ottley. Mr. Ottley himself undertook the research, the writing of the biography, and the annotation of the *Statement*. He completed his manuscript after nearly two years' work but was taken into the United States Naval Reserve before a final revision could be made. This revision, along with the checking of details and reading of proof, has been done by other members of the committee. Without the advantage that two years' research gives in familiarity with the subject, they have worked long and carefully, and it is hoped that errors have been kept to a minimum.

Although the committee acted as a group in preparing the book for publication, several members of the club both on and off the committee undertook special tasks. The revision, editing, and indexing were done largely by August Frugé and Neal Harlow. Mrs. Maloy had charge of the proofreading and was assisted by Miss Margaret Preston, Miss Evelyn Huston, Mrs. Marian Harlow, Mrs. Jean Bishop, and Walter E. Stoddard. Mrs. Grete Frugé translated parts of Lienhard's *Californien* and *Memoiren.* Mrs. Harrison was the committee's specialist in regard to binding. The decorations are by Neal Harlow. A number of other persons gave assistance when it was much needed.

A special word of thanks is due Mrs. Ruth C. Ottley, who assisted and encouraged her husband throughout his two years' work.

Committee for Publication Number Two

MRS. MIRIAM C. MALOY

MISS MARGARET E. PRESTON

MRS. MARGARET HARRISON

WALTER E. STODDARD

AUGUST FRUGÉ

NEAL HARLOW, *Acting Chairman*

June, 1943

Introduction

Albert L. Hurtado

THE HISTORY OF Sacramento and the California gold rush are inextricably linked with the name of John A. Sutter, the Swiss adventurer who in 1839 founded New Helvetia at the confluence of the American and Sacramento Rivers. The Sutter story is the stuff of American frontier lore. Sutter was, according to the familiar account, the sturdy founder of a settlement in the midst of Indians, protector of the homely immigrants who built their farms near Sutter's Fort, savior of the Donner Party, and destiny's instrument in the discovery of gold. Having brought the benefits of civilization and gold to California, so the popular story goes, ungrateful Californians stood by idly while squatters and speculators stripped Sutter of his land and wealth. After losing everything Sutter left the state that had abandoned him and lived his final years in Lititz, Pennsylvania, where he was regarded as a hero of the bygone golden frontier.

The more complete and more critical story of Sutter shows that he was largely responsible for his own problems.[1] A dissembling schemer who abandoned his family in Switzerland, Sutter fell from one financial disaster to another. He built his California empire on credit by making promises to pay that he had little realistic hope of fulfilling. New Helvetia was a house of cards about to crumble when Sutter's workmen found gold in the American River while they were building a sawmill. That fortuitous discovery set off a worldwide rush of hopeful goldseekers to California that temporarily forestalled Sutter's financial ruin. But Sutter could not live within his means or capitalize on the gold rush. His continued fecklessness in business matters, coupled with a serious drinking problem that fogged his judgment, preordained his eventual downfall. The California gold rush introduced a new kind of capitalist economy, in which creditors demanded payments for debts when they were due instead of Sutter's customary promises of future compensation. The land sharks and lawyers who now occupied the commercial waters of California fed on him without remorse.

John A. Sutter Jr., Sutter's eldest son, arrived in California about nine months after gold was discovered. Young Sutter, green as grass, was immediately plunged into the roiled waters of California land speculation and his father's questionable financial dealings. In a vain attempt to forestall his creditors and avoid foreclosure, Sutter Sr. signed over his property to his son. Horrified at the condition of his father's business affairs, the son tried to make things right and preserve something of his father's estate. It was a losing battle with many skirmishes along the way. Somehow, in the midst of these travails, Sutter Jr. managed to found Sacramento. Ill and disgusted with his experiences, young Sutter moved tc Mexico. Hoping to obtain compensation for the land that he lost, Sutter. Jr. returned to California in 1855 to give his lawyer a long "statement," which explained in detail how he and his father were swindled. This is an extraordinary document that reveals the seamy side of business and land speculation during the first great gold rush in the western United States.

This book was originally published by the Sacramento Book Collectors Club in 1943, under the title *Statement Regarding Early California Experiences*, and included a biography of Sutter Jr. Founded in 1939, the centennial year of Sutter's arrival in the Sacramento Valley, the Sacramento Book Collectors Club numbered among its members a few dedicated book lovers who appreciated old and rare books.[2] Not content to merely collect publications about Sacramento, the club soon determined to publish its own contributions to Sacramento history in limited editions. They followed in a distinguished tradition of fine press publications that is strong and deep in California.³ Quite naturally, the club's first publication, *A Faithful Translation of the Papers Respecting the Grant Made by Governor Alvarado to John A. Sutter*, was concerned with Sutter Sr.⁴ This first effort was some thirty-five pages long; the club printed only eighty copies, a minuscule edition even by fine press standards. The club's second publication, Sutter Jr.'s *Statement* and the accompanying biography, was a more ambitious venture by far. The completed book would stretch to more than 160 pages, so the complexity and expense of publication would be commensurately greater than that of the club's first volume.

But more importantly, the club's second book would entail a historical research project of serious proportions. Allan Ottley proposed to write the first substantial biography of Sutter Jr., a work that necessarily required research in primary sources. Ottley was not trained as a historian, nor had he published a book. Born in Vancouver, British Columbia, in 1909, Ottley moved to Santa Barbara with his parents when he was thirteen. He took a bachelor's degree in English and journalism from Santa Barbara State College in 1934, and then completed library training in Riverside. His first professional post took him from the arid desert to the rainy redwoods of Eureka, where he worked in the Humboldt County Library. Eventually he took a position with a WPA cataloging project at the California Department of Education, and moved from there to the Sacramento City Library. Ottley was among the book lovers who founded the Sacramento Book Collectors Club in 1939.⁵

Armed with a journalist's skepticism and a librarian's research skills, Ottley carried out his dual assignments as historical editor and biographer with keen enthusiasm, thoroughness, and good sense. The bulk of the sources that Ottley needed were close at hand, for the state library's California Room housed Sutter Jr.'s original "Statement" and a large corpus of materials relating to the Sutters, New Helvetia, Sacramento, and the gold rush. The University of California's Bancroft Library in Berkeley likewise had much valuable information. Wisely, Ottley recognized that additional documentary sources for his work were scattered from Mexico to Washington, D.C. He fired off letters to the National Archives, the Consular staff in Acapulco, and other people with private and official knowledge about Sutter Jr. when he was U.S. Consul in Acapulco. In addition he queried Sutter Jr.'s surviving relatives in Pennsylvania, Mexico, and California, thus adding oral history to his perspective on the Sutters.[6]

The project was an interesting diversion that combined Ottley's professional and avocational interests, but it was more than that. He was also laying the foundation for a permanent community of fine press work in Sacramento, perhaps a smaller version of the extensive fine printing establishment in San Francisco. The book was to be the first publication of the Sacramento Junior College (now Sacramento City College) training program for apprentice printers. This new program would not undertake commercial work but would "confine itself to fine typography," Ottley explained to one of his correspondents.[7] George Smisor, Ottley's friend, was in charge of the new program.[8]

Ottley contacted Sutter's relatives in San Francisco and Pennsylvania. He first heard from Howard Joseph Sutter Hull, whose pride in his Sutter lineage was evident in his signature. Hull, grandson of Sutter Jr., had a lot of practice in telling the family's history. Pennsylvania newspapermen frequently sought Hull's views on his grandfather and great grandfather.[9] Hull was born in Lititz in 1878, but moved to Acapulco with his mother (Sutter Jr.'s daughter) after the death of his father. He provided many helpful childhood memories and family reminiscences of his grandfather. Ottley was leery of some of the stories and cross-checked Hull with the National Archives.[10] In San Francisco Ottley interviewed Anna S. Young, Sutter Jr.'s daughter by his second wife. The question of "first" and "second" wives brought up a delicate matter. If Sutter Jr. married the woman who bore his first three children (including Hull's father), then why was there no record of the marriage? And how was he able to marry his "second" wife (Young's mother) without a divorce? "These two conflicting statements put me in a difficult situation,"

Ottley explained to one of his correspondents.[11] Bluntly stated, "One line of his descendants, then, must have been illegitimate," Ottley wrote privately, "and though it is a point on which I plan in no way to dwell at length in the biography of Don Juan, it is yet a rather important one."[12] Ottley never received clear and compelling evidence on this matter, but sided with the view that the "first" marriage was valid and the "second" was "left-handed."[13]

In addition to the delicate matter of legitimacy, Ottley had to contend with problems of time and distance. He enlisted aid wherever he could find it. One of his friends, the printer George Smisor, made an automobile trip from Mexico City to Acapulco to grub for information there. He dragooned Concha Hudson of the U.S. Consular staff in Acapulco to look into old Mexican records. Neal Harlow, on the State Library staff, accompanied Ottley to San Francisco to interview Anna Young. In the midst of all this the Imperial Japanese Navy attacked Pearl Harbor, plunged the United States into war, and made Ottley fodder for the draft. "Right now I am racing against time and the army in order to complete the book on your father," he explained to Young.[14] With the minions of the Selective Service hot on his trail, Ottley persevered at his task, cajoling Hudson to send him the information that he had requested. He confessed to "practically sitting on pins and needles in expectation of the goodness of your success in finding the information," he told her. "When you do, I shall certainly remember you in my prayers and the preface!"[15] He was as good as his word, at least as far as the preface was concerned.

Ottley won his race with the Army by joining the Naval Reserve, which eventually assigned him to active duty. Before his induction in late 1942, Ottley turned over his manuscript to the club's publication committee. With Ottley in the Navy and bound for the South Pacific, the final manuscript became a more collaborative effort than Ottley had expected. The committee included August Frugé and Neal Harlow, who took upon themselves the responsibility of preparing Ottley's manuscript for the printer. They judged that Ottley's writing "needed revision," Frugé recalled, and the two men "spent long evenings doing what I have since learned to decry as over-editing—recasting the author's sentences and paragraphs." Frugé suspected that Ottley never forgave them for their efforts, "Nor should he have, perhaps."[16] Nevertheless, Ottley was lucky in the editorial assistance that fell to him. Frugé parlayed his slender editorial experience with Ottley's manuscript into a job with the University of California Press and ultimately became the director of the press, a post that he held for thirty-two years. Harlow became a distinguished university librarian and eventually dean of the library school at Rutgers. Harlow also authored several books, including *California Conquered: War and Peace on the Pacific, 1846–1850* (Berkeley: Univ. of California Press, 1982). Harlow's spare line drawings of the Sacramento waterfront and Sutter's Fort adorn the present volume. By chance, the exigencies of the Great Depression had thrown all of these talented people together in Sacramento. Over-edited or not, Ottley's book retains a readable quality that is as fresh today as when it was first published sixty years ago.

Despite the editorial ministrations of Frugé and Harlow, Ottley's name deservedly belongs on the spine. Without Ottley, neither the original edition of this book nor the present volume would have been published. The book club published only 160 copies of the first edition—heroic work considering the shortages during World War II—and the book is now very rare. The republication of Sutter's statement brings to a broader audience the astonishing history of the founding of Sacramento. The preface to the first edition succinctly states the case for reissuing the book:

> It has the ring of truth about it, and its revelations are essential to a true understanding of the Sutter family and their part in the early history of Sacramento. Perhaps nowhere else is the unprincipled scramble for land in the Sacramento Valley so well portrayed.

This assessment is still essentially correct and applies to Ottley's biography of Sutter Jr. as well. In this volume we find a unique window into the world of gold-rush California and the men who scrambled to amass fortunes in land speculation.

Ottley's book, for such it is, is a tribute to him and the librarian-scholars who have contributed to California history for more than a century. When the war was over, Ottley returned to Sacramento and took a post in the state library's famed California Room, which holds the archives and rare books that chronicle the state's history. By 1953 he was supervisor of the California Room, a position that he held until his retirement in 1971. In the California Room Ottley was known by his initials, ARO. He continued to publish essays and books on California history. His last book, *John A. Sutter's Last Days: The Bidwell Letters* (1986), was a work of historical editing that, like his first book, concerned Sutter family history. It was the tenth publication of the Sacramento Book Collectors Club, and, like its predecessors, this slim volume was a compliment to the book-maker's art and to historical scholarship. The Book Club of California recognized Ottley's contributions with its coveted Oscar Lewis Award in 1999. ARO died the following year.[17]

Norman, Oklahoma

April 2002

Notes

I wish to thank Gary Kurutz of the California State Library for his assistance in preparing this introduction. And Don Pisani—friend, colleague, and fellow Sacramentan—read and offered valuable advice on the introduction.

1. The most recent scholarly appraisal of Sutter is Kenneth N. Owens, ed., *John Sutter and a Wider West* (Lincoln: University of Nebraska Press, 1994). There are many Sutter biographies of varying quality. The most reliable work is Richard Dillon, *Fool's Gold: The Decline and Fall of Captain John Sutter of California* (New York: Coward-McCann, 1967), republished under the same title by Western Tanager Press (Santa Cruz, 1981) and by the same press as *Captain John Sutter: Sacramento Valley's Sainted Sinner* in 1987. Also useful, though now outdated, is James Peter Zollinger, *Sutter: The Man and His Empire* (New York: Oxford University Press, 1939).

2. Martin Huff, preface to *John A. Sutter's Last Days: The Bidwell Letters*, ed. Allan R. Ottley (Sacramento: Sacramento Book Collectors Club, 1986), viii.

3. James D. Hart, *Fine Printing: The San Francisco Tradition* (Washington, D.C.: The Library of Congress, 1985); "The Sacramento Book Collectors Club," *The Book Club of California Quarterly Newsletter* 60, no. 2 (1995), 20.

4. John Plumbe and Neal Harlow, eds., *A Faithful Translation of the Papers Respecting the Grant Made by Governor Alvarado to John A. Sutter*, trans. W. E. P. Hartnell (Sacramento: Sacramento Book Collectors Club, 1942).

5. "1999 Oscar Lewis Awards," *The Book Club of California Quarterly News-Letter* 59, no. 3 (1999), 21–22.

6. See Ottley's correspondence in the John Augustus Sutter Jr. Collection, Box 315, California Room, State Library, Sacramento (cited hereafter as Sutter Jr. Collection).

7. Allan R. Ottley to Mrs. W. B. Young, October 15, 1942, Sutter Jr. Collection.

8. Allan R. Ottley to Mrs. W. B. Young, October 15, 1942, Sutter Jr. Collection. See Ottley's preface to the original edition, below.

9. See news clippings, Sutter, Information File, Lancaster County Historical Society, Lancaster, Pennsylvania.

10. Phillip Hamer, chief of the reference division, confirmed some of Hull's account. Hamer to Allan R. Ottley, August 27, 1941, Sutter Jr. Collection.

11. Ottley to Concha Hudson, January 27, 1942, Sutter Jr. Collection.

12. This text was crossed out on the back of Ottley's file copy of a letter. Ottley to Concha Hudson, February 16, 1942, Sutter Jr. Collection.

13. See Ottley, below, p. 68.

14. Ottley to Young, October 15, 1942, Sutter Jr. Collection.

15. Ottley to Hudson, October 15, 1942, Sutter Jr. Collection.

16. August Frugé, *A Skeptic Among Scholars: August Frugé on University Publishing* (Berkeley: University of California Press, 1993), 18–19.

17. "1999 Oscar Lewis Awards," *The Book Club of California Quarterly News-Letter* 59, no. 3 (1999), 21–22; "Ottley, Allan Robert," *Sacramento Bee*, December 31, 2000, Scene.

The Sutter Family and the
Origins of Gold-Rush Sacramento

Part I: *Biography of*
John A. Sutter, Jr.

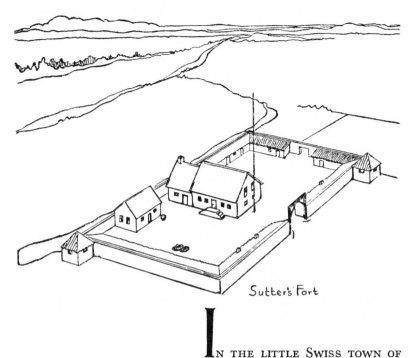

Sutter's Fort

I N THE LITTLE SWISS TOWN OF
BURGDORF, SOME TEN MILES FROM THE CITY OF BERN, A QUIET
WEDDING ON OCTOBER 24, 1826, UNITED ONE JOHANN AUGUST
Sutter and Anna Dübeld. It was a quiet wedding because it was a
necessary one, for the next day was born to the newlyweds their first
child, a son named after his father, Johann August Sutter, Jr.[1] The
little Johann's godparents were Gottlieb Friedrich Schlafli, husband
of his mother's sister; Jakob Friedrich Sutter, his father's only
brother; and Rosina Ris Dübeld, his grandmother.[2]

The young father, then twenty-three years old, was employed as a
clerk in the grocery store of Salzfaktor Aeschliemann in the Schmie-
dengasse, Burgdorf's main business street.[3] Before her marriage Anna
Sutter had assisted her widowed mother in the flourishing bakery and
restaurant left to them by Samuel Dübeld.[4]

---

[1] Zollinger, *Sutter,* p. 10.
[2] Howard Joseph Sutter Hull to the writer, Feb. 21, 1941.
[3] Zollinger, *Sutter,* pp. 9–11.
[4] *Ibid.,* p. 10.

[3]

Two years later, on August 28, 1828, Johann Sutter set himself up in business, probably with the financial aid of his mother-in-law. He opened a draper's shop and dry goods store in Burgdorf. Although he worked hard, his heart was not in the business, and in May, 1832, his creditors forced him into an arrangement for paying his mounting debts. Still the business faltered. At last, faced with debtors' prison, Sutter secretly secured a passport, dated May 13, 1834, and slipped out of Switzerland forever. One jump ahead of the police he crossed into France, made for the sea-coast, and took the first ship to America.[5]

Few escapes have had such momentous results. Not many years later this obscure little tradesman was a great figure in the almost legendary land of California, transacting business with foreign governments and dabbling in intrigue and war. One of the men in his employ made the great gold discovery, and his own son founded the capital city of a great new state. But all this lay secretly in the future.

Left behind in Burgdorf were Sutter's wife and five children. When her mother died, Frau Sutter's share of the estate was seized to secure her husband's debts; and since she could not earn enough to support her family, she was forced to accept the aid of her sisters. Young August was not yet eight years old.[6] Little is known of the trying years that followed for the deserted family. While John Sutter was skipping about the New World — New York, Westport (the newborn Kansas City), Santa Fé, Fort Vancouver, Honolulu, Sitka, Monterey, New Helvetia — creating for himself a bogus military title, trading to the Southwest, and finally building an empire on the Pacific Coast, his family back in Burgdorf was struggling desperately for respectable existence. It is said that young August was raised by Martin Birman, who also acted as legal adviser for the family.[7]

In 1839, five years after leaving Switzerland, John Sutter arrived from the Sandwich Islands by way of Alaska, at the tiny village of Yerba Buena in California. A few scattered buildings close by the shore (now Montgomery Street) comprised the settlement. Hardly

---

[5] *Ibid.,* pp. 11–15.

[6] *Ibid.,* p. 16.

[7] Blaise Cendrars to Reginaldo R. Sutter, Nov. 8, 1926.

fifty persons lived there.[8] Sutter, as much as any other man, was to be responsible for the growth of this drowsy village into the roaring city of San Francisco.

But now, only visions of an empire to be carved out of the California wilderness shone in his eyes. At Monterey, the capital of Alta California, Governor Alvarado gave him permission to ascend the unfamiliar Sacramento River and settle on some suitable stretch of land along its banks. In a year the settler should return to Monterey for his papers of Mexican citizenship and eventually for title to his chosen lands. At once he bustled about with preparations. On August 9, 1839, with two small chartered schooners and a four-oared pinnace, he set out from Yerba Buena for the Sacramento, and after eight days, entered a tributary stream, the American. Here he established himself on a small rise two or three miles from its mouth. With him were three white men, an Indian boy, and ten Kanakas, including two women.[9]

From this small nucleus sprang New Helvetia, named by Sutter after the country of his birth. Sutter's Fort was the outpost and later became the center of considerable settlement in the wide valley of the Sacramento. A year after leaving Monterey, Sutter returned to secure Mexican naturalization papers, and on June 18, 1841, Governor Alvarado gave him title to any eleven broad leagues of land he might select within a thirty-three-league area.[10]

Surrounded by these princely acres, he now remembered the family he had deserted in Switzerland. Unable to send them the funds they needed so badly, he still wished to show them that he was prospering in the New World. In 1843 John Bidwell, probably his most

---

[8] Bancroft, *Calif.*, III, 709–711.

[9] Various dates are given for this journey. Davis (*Sixty Years in Calif.*, p. 17), who was captain of one of the schooners, Bancroft (*Calif.*, IV, 130), and Dana (*Sutter of Calif.*, p. 77) all agree on Aug. 9 as the starting date. Davis declares that eight days were consumed in reaching the site selected. This would place the date of arrival on the 17th. Bancroft (*Calif.*, IV, 131) thinks they arrived about the 16th and scoffs at the oft-told story that it was eight days before the party even found the mouth of the Sacramento River, but Dana (*op. cit.*, pp. 78–79) stretches it to nine days, plus another two ascending the river. Zollinger (*Sutter*, p. 67) gives Aug. 13 or 14 as the date of the founding of the settlement.

[10] Zollinger, *Sutter*, pp. 79–80, 89, 133.

reliable and trusted employee, was asked to do some lettering on a map of the New Helvetia grant *made on thin paper for the purpose, as he informed me, of sending it to his family in Europe.*[11] It is unlikely that the hard-pressed family found much comfort in this map of a prairie wilderness.

Although Sutter was unable to help support his wife and children, he did seek to brighten their future. Since it was so easy to obtain free land, why not secure a tract for his family? Why not take up the remainder of that vast unoccupied territory from which he had picked his own choice eleven leagues? Manuel Jimeno, Governor Micheltorena's secretary, declared that as early as 1843 or 1844, Sutter petitioned in the name of his son for an extension of his land. The governor waited only for an opportunity to make a personal inspection of the Sacramento Valley before granting this and a number of other petitions, but political disturbances never allowed him to make the visit.[12] Sutter placed the blame on Jimeno. In the latter part of 1844 he wrote to Hartnell,[13] an English merchant at Monterey, that *my request however has been turned down by Mr. Jimeno because "my son is not here and because he is not naturalised,"* etc. *I would not say anything if I were asking for something new; but I have a title to this very land I only wish to have the lower part upon which the fort is situated transferred in favor of my son.*[14]

In 1845 there came an opportunity to gain more land—but at a price. For some time dissatisfaction with Micheltorena had been growing and particularly with the ruffians he had brought from Mexico in his military force. By late 1844 preparations for a revolt were well under way, and on the first of the new year Sutter, with some two hundred armed American pioneers and Indians, marched to join the governor's troops against the rebels, who were mustering in southern California. At Santa Barbara, on February 5, 1845, the

---

[11] *U. S.* v. *Sutter,* p. 557.

[12] *Ibid.,* pp. 12–13.

[13] William E. P. Hartnell, an Englishman, came to California in 1822 as agent of a Lima firm. He married, became a Mexican citizen, and held a number of public offices at Monterey, the capital. He was always close to the Mexican government and in 1844 was inspector and acting administrator of the custom house. (Bancroft, *Calif.,* III, 777.)

[14] Sutter to Hartnell, Dec. 13, 1844, in Vallejo, *Documentos,* XXXIV, ms. 81.

governor, in return for Sutter's loyalty, services, and the great expense which the campaign was causing him, granted his request for the *sobrante* or marginal lands remaining in the thirty-three leagues.

Whereas Don Juan Augustus Sutter [the document read], *a Mexican naturalized citizen, and his son, John A. Sutter, have solicited for the personal benefit of themselves and family the surplus of land within his rancho, named New Helvetia. . . . I have conceded to them the mentioned land, declaring in them the ownership thereof by these presents. . . .* [Signed] MANUEL MICHELTORENA[15]

Of the campaign itself, it need only be said that Micheltorena was forced to surrender, he and his men were banished to Mexico, and Sutter was lucky to escape with his life from the wrath of the Californians. The campaign cost him $8000,[16] a rather high price for the new property judged by the prevailing rates.

The apparent anomaly of Sutter, Jr., receiving land while still a minor and living abroad, became a disputed point years later, when the United States Land Commission was challenging the validity of all Mexican land grants in California. During the first review of Sutter's claims, in 1855, the question of young Sutter's right to acquire land was raised. After hearing considerable argument on both sides, Commissioners R. A. Thompson and S. B. Farwell confirmed the Sutter grants, with this ruling:

The fact that he was a minor and non-resident at the time of the grant [sobrante lands] *is fully established by the testimony, but we have been unable to find any provision of the Mexican law prohibiting grants to minors; indeed the contrary may be inferred from the 16th article of the regulation of November 21st, 1828, which authorizes grants to be made of the unappropriated lands to the children of the adjoining proprietors, without any restriction as to minority. With regard to residence of John A. Sutter, jr., we think that it is very clear that the 15th section of the law of August, 1824, cited by the law agent, does not apply in the present case. The Mexican law prescribing rules for giving letters of naturalization provides, in the 8th article,*

---

[15] *U. S.* v. *Sutter,* pp. 81–82.
[16] Zollinger, *Sutter,* p. 156.

that the naturalization of the husband and head of the family shall be considered as naturalizing the wife, and the minor or unemancipated children; and again, in the 9th article, it declares that children of Mexican citizens, born out of [the] republic, shall be considered as born in it. These provisions conferred on John A. Sutter, jr., the same rights of citizenship which were possessed by his father; and under the rule which obtains both in the civil and common law, making the domicile of the father, in contemplation of law, the domicile of the minor children, he was as capable of acquiring real property as any other citizen of the republic.[17]

Thus, John Sutter, Jr., while still in Switzerland, was a considerable landowner in California. His possessions yielded him nothing then and, as we shall see, very little in the future.

After his unhappy experience in the Micheltorena war, Sutter returned to New Helvetia and sought, by hard work and imaginative planning, to regain the loss sustained in military equipment, horses, and supplies. By 1847 his frontier establishment was a beehive of activity. His men sowed wheat and planted orchards, cured salmon and trapped beaver. Leather tanning, distilling, blacksmithing, and building went on constantly under the founder's watchful supervision. He established Hock Farm on the Feather River and built a large ranch house, while down the Sacramento River several miles from the mouth of the American he laid out a little town called Sutterville.

In 1846 a group of discontented American settlers, encouraged by the timely presence of Lieutenant John Frémont and his unusually well armed exploring expedition, staged what is known as the Bear Flag revolt and captured the town of Sonoma. This fighting merged into the Mexican War. American sea and land forces completed the conquest of California and began to stabilize the country under firm military rule. This was the situation when Sutter wrote to John Marsh, an American recluse living on a ranch near Mt. Diablo.

Yesterday I received at last some letters of my family and with the greatest of pleasure I see that my eldest Son, 20 Years and 6 Months

---

[17] *U. S.* v. *Sutter*, p. 134.

old is on his way to California and will be here in about 6 or 7
Months, his education is finished, likewise his aprentisage in one of
the first counting houses in Switzerland,[18] *he speaks and writes sev-*
eral languages, and no doubt will be an able Clerk. My Family re-
mains in Switzerland a year or two longer till the two younger Sons
have received their education complete, the second [Emil Victor] *is*
in a celebrated Agricultural Institut, the 3th [William Alphonse] *is*
in a Military school or Academie as Cadet.[19] *The education of my*
Daughter about 19 years old is completed likewise, it was a great
pleasure to read all their letters out which I can judge how the[y]
received their education and was to my greatest Satisfaction.[20]

The eminent counting house in which August received his training
was actually one of the smaller business houses in Burgdorf, declares
Zollinger, who has unearthed much new material on the Sutter family. The *celebrated Agricultural Institut* was of doubtful renown,
and the *Military school or Academie* was only an ordinary private
school.[21]

Sutter kept his friends posted regularly regarding the movements
of his family, a fact which might indicate that he looked forward to
seeing them once more, but his desertion of them and his long in-
difference to their needs do not support this supposition. Perhaps
he merely liked to write letters. *I expect my family here in about five*
months, he wrote in a note of May 4, 1848, to Heinrich Thomen;[22]
and a week later he sent the news to J. F. Romie, his Monterey
tailor: *In five months I expect my family, which will come over the*
Rocky Mountains with some of our relatives and friends. This will
produce a considerable change in New Helvetia.[23]

First of Sutter's family to reach California was John August, Jr.,

---

[18] Sutter, writing to John Jacob Jenny of Basel in 1880 declared: "August,
the eldest, had already served his apprenticeship with the firm of Schnel in
Burgdorf." (Quoted in Hull to the writer, Feb. 21, 1941.)

[19] Alphonse actually served as a captain in William Walker's filibustering
expedition to Nicaragua in 1855. (Greene, *Filibuster,* p. 122.)

[20] Quoted in Zollinger, *Sutter,* p. 189.

[21] *Ibid.,* pp. 6, 190.

[22] *Calif. Hist. Soc. Quarterly,* XI (1932), 42.

[23] Sutter to Romie, May 12, 1848, in *Sacramento Bee,* June 9, 1930.

who arrived in San Francisco on September 14, 1848, aboard the
ship *Huntress,* just short of one hundred fifty days from New York.[24]
It was indeed a timely arrival for this slim young man of twenty-
two. Several months before, his father had needed lumber and had
sent one James Marshall up the American River to build a sawmill.
There, one January morning, in little Coloma Valley, Marshall picked
up some shiny, yellow flakes that dotted the bed of the tail race. Odd
bits of something. Soft? He creased one with his nail. Malleable? The
hammer beat it flat. Gold! Gold from the creek bed! Gold for the
digging and washing! The mill was forgotten and all it meant to
John Sutter. How vain the attempt at secrecy! Eager ears caught the
word down in the big valley and in the settlement by the bay. The
ranchero turned his horse eastward. The merchant closed his shop
and followed. The sailor deserted his ship. The farmer and the trapper, the soldier, the doctor, and the lawyer hurried to the fabulous
mountain creeks.[25]

The first wave of a great tide of gold-hungry men was already on
its way when young August set foot on California soil. Seeing this
human wave sweeping up the Sacramento River to his father's fort
and pressing on beyond, the young man little realized, perhaps, that
he was witnessing the beginning of a movement he was soon to know
with bitter sorrow.

Sutter must have looked on his son's arrival with mixed feelings.
His empire was already beginning to crumble. Employees had deserted for the mines, leaving the fields untended and half-tanned
leather putrefying in the vats. On their way to the mines the gold
seekers trampled his crops and even shot his cattle for food. A strong
and determined man was needed, and Sutter was never that except
in his dealings with the Indians. Perhaps, he felt, August would be
that man.[26]

Even this possibility could not dispel the father's deep-seated re-

[24] *Californian,* Sept. 16, 1848.
[25] For description of the beginning of the gold rush, see Bancroft, *Calif.,* VI,
52–66.
[26] For description of the effect of the gold rush on activities at the Fort, see
ibid., VI, 103–105.

sentment of his eldest son, a feeling which he never altogether lost. All too often he must have remembered that it was the imminent arrival of this child twenty-two years before, that had trapped him into an undesired marriage. And that marriage had not only trussed up his gay and irresponsible spirit in prosaic draper's cloth, but had eventually contributed to a shameful business failure. *Indeed*, writes Zollinger, *there was buried in him a deep, primordial, and largely unconscious hatred against this fatal child.*[27] Perhaps, too, the lord of New Helvetia was ashamed to face the deserted son, now little more than a stranger. In any event, Sutter was conveniently absent at the mines, evidently drinking more than mining,[28] when his son stepped from the little river schooner *Sacramento* on to the *Embarcadero* and trudged the dusty way up to the Fort.

In his *Statement Regarding Early California Experiences*, printed as the second part of this book, Sutter, Jr., shows his astonishment at the negligent way in which the establishment was managed. He, who knew so well the desperate need of his family in old Helvetia, was distressed at the inefficiency and wasteful disorder that he found in the new.[29] It is not surprising, therefore, that he promptly took advantage of a fortunate circumstance to bring the tottering empire under his own management.

Sutter had never completed payment for the Fort Ross and Bodega establishments, purchased from the Russian American Fur Company in 1841. For two years the Russians had been pressing him for installments that should have been paid by 1845, and now they were ready to attach his property. The situation had already reached a critical stage, when George McKinstry wrote to Pierson B. Reading from New Helvetia on November 2, 1846.

I arrived at this place on Oct. 19th. Capt. Sutter has received me with the utmost kindness and wishes me to assist him in his business as long as I wish. The Russian American Company have attached all the real estate of your friend Capt. Sutter to secure their debt of

---

[27] Zollinger, *Sutter,* p. 14.

[28] Lienhard, *Pioneer,* pp. 149, 154, 155–156.

[29] For an eyewitness picture of disorderly conditions at the Fort, see *ibid.,* pp. 160–161, 164–165.

$27,000 at the request of Capt. Sutter and Mr. Sinclair, the Alcalde. I have accepted the appointment of Sheriff and Inspector of this district and serve the attachment. In this part of the country it is only known by us three. I have written to Mr. Hastings[30] and enclosed him the copy and asked his opinion. Mr. Leidesdorff[31] writes that the Company only wants to prevent the sale of lands until their attachment has been paid. I presume it was brought about by Leidesdorff although in his letter he deems it at the request of Capt. Sutter. I have written to Commodore Stockton[32] at Monterey offering him the Fort and a sufficient quantity of land, and referred him to you for description of place and price. Capt. Sutter will write you on the subject by Mr. Burrows. He appears to be anxious to sell it and retire to his farm on the Feather River. It is, of course, unnecessary to ask you to lend your assistance in effecting the sale.[33]

It was only the fortunate arrival of August and a hasty transfer of the entire Sutter property from father to son that precluded a foreclosure. The transfer took place at the Fort on October 14. *For and in consideration of fifty thousand dollars . . . to me in hand paid by John A. Sutter, jr.,* the old pioneer conveyed to his son all his Sacramento Valley property, the Fort Ross property consisting of approximately six leagues, the sawmill and a square mile of land at Coloma, and a lot in San Francisco.[34] By a second instrument, made at the same time, he transferred for a stated $15,000 his personal property, which included fifteen hundred horses, fifty mules, six hundred cattle, twenty saddles and bridles, and the schooner *Sacramento*.[35] That the Sutters were not deliberately trying to cheat the Russians is clearly

---

30 Lansford W. Hastings, a lawyer, who was interested with Sutter in developing the town of Sutterville. (Bancroft, *Calif.*, III, 778.)

31 William Alexander Leidesdorff, a pioneer of 1841, was in Oct. 1845 appointed U. S. vice-consul by T. O. Larkin, U. S. consul in California. (Bancroft, *Calif.*, IV, 711.)

32 Commodore Robert F. Stockton came to California as captain of the ship *Congress* in 1846 and succeeded Commodore Sloat in command of our Pacific squadron. Until Jan. 1847, he was also military governor of California. He was one of the energetic leaders in the American conquest of the territory during the Mexican War. (Bancroft, *Calif.*, V, 735.)

33 Quoted in *New Helvetia Diary*, p. xxiii.

34 Sacramento County, *Deed Books*, vol. C, pp. 351–353.

35 *Ibid.*, vol. A, pp. 3–4.

indicated by the *Statement* and proved by the final payment to the company's agent. Peter H. Burnett, who became young Sutter's agent, also confirmed this on two occasions.[36]

Just one day after the transfer, the young Swiss joined with Major Samuel J. Hensley, Major Pierson B. Reading, and Jacob R. Snyder in establishing the firm of Hensley, Reading & Co. Each was to furnish three thousand dollars in *gold dust, or grain gold* or its equivalent as capital. It is interesting to see what contributions were made by August in lieu of cash:

John A. Sutter Jr. binding himself to procure suitable buildings at Capt Sutter's Fort for the operations of the aforesaid Company. Also, to procure the exclusive use of the launch named Sacramento *for the use of the aforesaid Company as long as it may exist.*

Also, to obtain a quantity of land for the use of the aforesaid Company; said land extending from the mouth of the River known as the American Fork, one thousand yards down the Sacramento River, and a distance of three hundred yards back, from said Sacramento River and on the East side, having the exclusive privilege to erect houses thereon and cut such timber as may be required for the use of the aforesaid Company in any of their opperations. Also all ferry rights for ever in my name.

Also, to have the use and entire control of the ferry, and its appurtenances, at the Embarcadero, known as Capt. Sutter's Landing, at the expiration of the term for which it has been rented, to the present proprietors Mr. McDougal & Co., at the same rate now rented, and so long as the Company may exist.

Each partner to devote his entire time and attention to the business of the Company and not enter into any trade, but that connected with the Firm unless by the consent of all parties, and to perform such a part of the duties, trade, or business, as may tend to advance the interest of the Company.

The stipulations herein contained in refference to John A. Sutter

---

[36] His *Recollections,* p. 288, and again in a letter of Jan. 18, 1894, to Sutter, Jr., in which he says that the transfer of property was designed "only to temporarily delay one creditor for the ultimate benefit of all, that our object was to pay all the debts as early as possible." (Sutter, Jr., papers.)

Jr procuring suitable buildings at Capt. Sutter's Fort for the use of the aforesaid Company, Also, that regarding a certain quantity of land at the Embarcadero on Capt Sutter Landing, Also, the Ferry's as herein mentioned; All and Singular to be considered as equivalent to the amount of Capital furnished by each of the aforesaid partners, Hensley, Reading & Snyder.[37]

On November 1, a codicil was added, amending particularly the contribution of land:

The parties to the above instrument since signing have agreed to release the conditions relative to the use of the land and ferries on the Sac River as herein mentioned with the condition that it is appropriated to the city of Sacramento for her own use and benefit, which City is to be laid out along said River.[38]

The new firm was soon doing business at the Fort. One of the first clerks hired was James King of William, a young banker from Washington, D.C., whose later newspaper campaign against vice and corruption and his consequent murder led to the formation of San Francisco's famous second Vigilance Committee in 1856.

August had no sooner taken title to New Helvetia than his father rushed off once more to Coloma, perhaps to get away from a wronged son's reproachful eye and perhaps to forget the loss of his empire. He established a business in miners' supplies under the firm name of Sutter, Hastings & Co., but he was no better business man there than at the Fort. The company was an immediate and heavy money loser and before long was ten thousand dollars in debt.[39]

Sutter, Jr., immediately began raising money to pay off the obligations of the debt-ridden empire he had taken over from his father. Typical were his dealings with M. G. Vallejo, of Sonoma. In February, 1848, Captain Sutter had refused to sell Vallejo a still, because he intended to use it as soon as the Coloma mill was finished. Not so the

---

[37] "Excerpts from the Memorial of the Society of California Pioneers to Major Jacob Rink Snyder," Soc. Calif. Pioneers, *Quarterly*, VIII (1931), 211, 213.

[38] *Ibid.*, p. 213.

[39] Zollinger, *Sutter*, p. 269. "I was engaged," wrote Sutter later, "in a mercantile firm in Coloma, which I left in January, 1849 . . . with many sacrifices." ("The Discovery of Gold in California," *Hutchings' Calif. Magazine*, II [1857], 198.)

son. *My father told me some days ago,* August wrote to Vallejo, *that you, Sir, wishes to buy his distillery apparatus and having just nowe no use for it, I take the liberty to offer it to you for the moderate price of 400$.* Vallejo snapped it up.[40] And in September, 1849, he asked Vallejo to run down one *Señor St. Clair who went away from her[e] in my absence* and collect from him money due the Sutters.[41]

Meanwhile the young Swiss clerk found that he had other problems on his hands. A group of noisy loiterers who hung about the Fort sponging on the Sutters kept life in a constant turmoil. *Drunkenness seemed to be the daily condition of everyone, even men who should have remained sober,* lamented Lienhard, one of Captain Sutter's most trusted employees. *Young Sutter, whom I genuinely admired, was a man of moderate tastes, and this crude wild life must have been abhorrent to him.*[42]

On one occasion a number of these hoodlums were carelessly amusing themselves with firecrackers, letting some fall on the dry shingles of a roof and others explode at the feet of a panic-stricken horse. When Sutter called them fools and ordered them to stop, one of them swaggered up and defied him to repeat what he had said. August, disconcerted, replied *that he did not mean anything by it, but had merely been afraid that the fort would be set on fire.*[43]

Another time the young man, callow and unused to the frontier roughness of his new environment, met with a more serious upset. While his father was away at the mines August took over his duties as Indian sub-agent for the Sacramento and San Joaquin Valleys.[44] One day several Indians complained that white men from the Fort had stolen a horse of theirs. Young Sutter immediately accused one of the suspected men, and received the sullen answer that the horse had

[40] Sutter to Vallejo, Feb. 10, 1848; Sutter, Jr., to Vallejo, Dec. 28, 1848, and Apr. 23, 1849, in Vallejo, *Documentos,* XII, mss. 332, 357; XIII, ms. 14.

[41] Sutter, Jr., to Vallejo, Sept. 3, 1849, in *ibid.,* XIII, ms. 25. St. Clair was probably the Scotsman, John Sinclair, who had many dealings with the elder Sutter, lived on the nearby Del Paso Rancho, and in 1846–49 was *alcalde* of the Sacramento district. (Bancroft, *Calif.,* V, 721.)

[42] Lienhard, *Pioneer,* p. 164.

[43] *Ibid.,* p. 165.

[44] He was appointed in 1847 at an annual salary of $750 and had power only to admonish and look after the Indians. (Bancroft, *Calif.,* VII, 477.)

been stolen first by the Indians. Sutter believed the man was lying, and, in spite of Lienhard's efforts to dissuade him, he continued to uphold the Indians' case. Soon he was engaged in a rough-and-tumble fight with the accused fellow. Lienhard claims that he tried to pull young Sutter away but was prevented by the justice of the peace, armed with a club. The two fighters fell to the ground, Sutter's opponent gaining the upper hand. Lienhard writes, *I advised Sutter to stop. He consented, but only after his face was badly scratched. If he had listened to me in the beginning, he would have saved himself this embarrassment, for he had had little experience with men of this type.*[45]

It was a bitter incident to August, and he immediately shut himself up in his father's room. Lienhard tried to console him and offered helpful advice. When the elder Sutter returned to the Fort he decided to reprimand everyone concerned.[46]

About this time August had some difficulty with Charles E. Pickett, known as Philosopher Pickett, one of the traders in the Fort. Pickett and the elder Sutter were on friendly terms, and it may be that the trader sought to use his friendship with the father to obtain special privileges from the son. Whatever the cause, young Sutter rented Pickett's quarters from under him, compelling the Philosopher to move to another room. Pickett was furious. He instituted a civil action against the elder Sutter, but the case was dismissed for lack of cause by *Alcalde* John Sinclair. Pickett never forgot the matter and for years he insisted that the Sutters owed him for the loss he suffered.[47]

The Captain's son, however, soon had projects outside the Fort to occupy his mind, for shortly after taking over his father's property he began to think of establishing a new town near the river. Supplies for the mines were being landed at the *Embarcadero*, on the bank of the Sacramento just below the mouth of the American River, and there was need for a business community at the bustling waterfront. He had the project in mind as early as November 1, 1848, and encour-

---

[45] Lienhard, *Pioneer*, pp. 199–200.
[46] *Ibid.*, p. 200.
[47] Powell, *Philosopher Pickett*, p. 46.

aged by Sam Brannan and other traders at the Fort, he decided to lay out a town.

Fortunately for the city of Sacramento the elder Sutter was snow-bound in the mountains. For several years he himself had been pro-moting a town at the hog farm, on rising ground some three miles below the confluence of the two rivers. He called it Sutterville, and, as early as October, 1845, he wrote to Thomas O. Larkin, United States consul at Monterey, that *after the rains a new city will be founded,* adding that Prudon was planning to leave his court at Sonoma to build a hotel at Sutterville.[48]

Sutterville was a long time a-borning. Under date of February 7, 1846, the *New Helvetia Diary* states that *Capt. Hastings & Bidwell finished laying out the town.* Several more references appear during the next two years, and finally on May 13, 1848, *Mr. Bidwell re-turned from Sutter'sville where he was surveying.*[49] Sutter was still hopeful on May 4, 1848. In a letter reporting the gold discovery to Heinrich Thomen, he wrote: *You shall see that Sutterville will im-mediately become a town.*[50] Even more enthusiastically he wrote to J. F. Romie eight days later: *Our new town, Suttersville, will soon be next in size to San Francisco among Californian towns.*[51]

But Sutterville never rose out of its open fields. Today its area is a small-farm and residential suburb of the Sacramento his son founded, remembered only in Sutterville Road, a long artery running eastward from the Sacramento River.

Ignoring his father's projected town, August made prompt plans for his own settlement. Hiring William H. Warner of the U. S. Topo-graphical Engineers to do the surveying, he gave him a munificent sixteen dollars a day and several assistants to lay out streets on the broad grassy prairie stretching away from the river. Warner had re-cently come from the mines with Lieutenants William T. Sherman and E. O. C. Ord and was camped with them near the Fort. He completed

[48] Sutter to Larkin, Oct. 8, 1845, in Larkin, *Documents,* III, ms. 315.

[49] See entries under June 11, 18, 22, July 12, 14, 1847; Feb. 13, Apr. 6, May 7, 8, 11, 13, 1848.

[50] Quoted in *Calif. Hist. Soc. Quarterly,* XI (1932), 42.

[51] Sutter Collection, May 12, 1848.

a map in December, 1848, but continued to survey into the new year.[52]

Heinrich Lienhard, who owned lots in the undeveloped Sutterville, writes that when the son sought his opinion of the new site, he advised in favor of it. He continues: *I now committed an error which I afterward regretted. I advised against the name Suttersville and recommended the name Sacramento City, which he did give to the city. Had I thought at the time of Sutter's* [the father's] *vanity, his name, of which he was very proud though undeservedly, would now be forever linked with the city. However, I can console myself for this sin of omission with the knowledge that Sacramento owes her name to me.*[53] The name was used as early as November 1, 1848, in the Hensley, Reading codicil, and by December 28, young Sutter was dating his letters from Sacramento instead of from New Helvetia.[54]

On that day he sold to Hensley, Reading & Co. for sixty-five hundred dollars four river-front lots in the block bounded by Front, Second, I and J Streets; also a row of adobe buildings in the Fort and the southeast corner of land outside the Fort bounded by the east gate, 28th Street, L Street and the south gate.[55]

August had just begun to sell lots when Peter H. Burnett arrived in Sacramento. Burnett was an Oregon lawyer drawn to California by the gold discovery, and he had already tried his hand at mining on the Yuba River. Into the hands of this man, later to become California's first civil governor, young Sutter placed, on December 30, 1848, all the property to be sold in the new town. Thus the state's future capital city was born.[56] If August was the father of Sacramento, then Burnett may be said to have been its wet nurse. *I had*

---

[52] Stoddard, "William H. Warner," *Engineerogram,* I (1939), 3–4; Bancroft, *Calif.,* VI, 447.

[53] Translated from his *Californien,* p. 231. Sutter, Jr., in his *Statement* says that the "name of Sacramento city was proposed to me by Capt. Warner, Mr. Brannan, and a great many others."

[54] Sutter to Vallejo, Feb. 10, 1848, and Sutter, Jr., to Vallejo, Dec. 28, 1848, in Sutter Collection. In November, too, both Brannan and Pickett had begun using the name Sacramento in their newspaper advertisements. (*Calif. Star & Californian,* Nov. 18, 1848.)

[55] Sacramento County, *Deed Books,* vol. A, pp. 5–6.

[56] *Ibid.,* vol. A, p. 40; vol. C, p. 250.

only been at the Fort a few days, Burnett wrote years later, *when John A. Sutter, Jr. . . . proposed to employ me as his attorney and agent. The terms agreed upon between us were such as his mercantile partner, Major Hensley, thought fair and just. I was to attend to all of his law business of every kind, sell the lots in Sacramento City, and collect the purchase money; and for these services I was to receive one fourth of the gross proceeds arising from the sale of city lots.*[57] To facilitate Burnett's agency, the founder gave him his power of attorney on January 18, 1849, to sell *at such prices as he my said attorney in his discretion may think right.*[58]

Morton Matthew McCarver, another Oregonian attracted to California, and a Sacramento delegate to the Constitutional Convention, has also been given credit for the conception and original planning of Sacramento City. According to a biography written by his son-in-law, *McCarver suggested the laying out of a town and sale of lots, and as the Sutters knew nothing of that kind of business, offered to manage the enterprise for them. The offer was accepted, and an engineer named William H. Warner was employed to survey and plat the town in the fall of 1848. . . . About the time the Sacramento plat was completed, in December, McCarver's old associate, Peter H. Burnett came along. . . . Becoming acquainted with young Sutter, he secured for himself the business that had been promised to McCarver. . . . He was a lawyer and McCarver was not. . . . Gen. McCarver was astounded at what he regarded as the duplicity and treachery of his former friend, Burnett.*[59] No other evidence appears to substantiate this claim.

The need for the new town was evidenced by the immediate and rapid development of Sacramento City. Early in January, 1849, upon the completion of the map, Burnett began to sell lots in the oak-dotted fields. *There were then,* he wrote, *only two houses near the* embarcadero. *One was a rude log-cabin, in which a drinking saloon was kept; and the other, also a log-cabin, was occupied by an*

[57] His *Recollections,* p. 287.
[58] Sacramento County, *Powers of Attorney,* vol. A, pp. 25–26; Sacramento County, *Deed Books,* vol. A, pp. 40–41.
[59] Prosch, *McCarver and Tacoma,* pp. 54–55.

excellent old man named Stewart and his family. Nearly all the first
sales were of lots near the Fort; but toward the end of January the
lots near the river began to sell most rapidly. The prices for lots in the
same locality were fixed and uniform; and I made it an inflexible
rule not to lower the prices for speculators, thus preventing a monop-
oly of the lots. I discouraged the purchase of more than four lots by
any one person. I said to those who applied for lots: "You can well
afford to buy four lots, and can stand the loss without material injury
if the city should fail; but, if it should succeed, you will make enough
profit on this number." This moderate and sensible advice satisfied
the purchasers, and built up the city. The terms were part cash and
part on time, the purchaser giving his note for the deferred payment, and
receiving a bond for a warranty deed when the note should be paid.[60]

Before the general sale of lots began, John Sutter, Jr., on January
2, made several gifts to the city he was founding. All streets and
alleys were to be kept for public use except those within the Fort.
Until said city shall be incorperated & city authorityes established
Frount street shall be subject to the exclusive use of the owners of lots
frunting on said frunt street in such man[n]er that the owners of said
lot or part of a lot fronting on said street shall have the exclusive use
of all the ground lyinge immediately opposite his lot or part of a lot,
and betwene such lot or part of lot & the River. All cross streets, such
as L and M, *shall remain at all times open for Public use.*[61]

Then, with magnificent civic generosity, he gave ten well placed
squares *for the public use of the inhabitance of said city to be ap-*
plyed to such public purposes as the future inco[r]perated authoritys
of said city from tim[e] to time declare and deturmine. And, lastly, he
reserved all the ferry rights for himself and his heirs.[62] The inter-
pretation of *exclusive use* of the river front and of *the public use of*
the inhabitance has been the subject of considerable controversy in
later years.

---

[60] Burnett, *Recollections,* pp. 293–294.

[61] Five blocks of M St., recently renamed Capitol Ave., have been closed for
years by the state capitol and grounds.

[62] Sacramento County, *Deed Books,* vol. A, pp. 164–165. Reprinted from time
to time in the Sacramento newspapers; see particularly *Union,* May 13, 1903,
and *Bee,* June 22, 1914, May 1, 1917, and June 26, 1933.

The initial public sale of lots was announced at San Francisco in California's only newspaper, in these words:

PUBLIC AUCTION
Of Town Lots in the new Town of Sacramento,
Will take place at Sutter's Fort, in said town, on Monday the eighth day of January, 1849. The advantages which this sale now offers to merchants or mechanics wishing a residence near the mines, are too evident for comment. This sale also includes the lots lying at Sutter's Embarcadero, which is included in the town.

Maps of the new town can be seen at Maj. P. B. Reading's office in San Francisco, or at the proprietor's in Sutter's Fort.

Dec. 2, 1848.[63]

On the appointed day the auction was held, and Burnett reported that business continued *remarkably brisk*. The whirl of sales raised a new problem, for it was soon recognized that some form of local government was needed to provide official acknowledgment and record of the deeds. Consequently, a public meeting was held early in January, and Henry A. Schoolcraft, an ex-sergeant of the New York Volunteers, was elected first magistrate and recorder for the District of Sacramento.[64]

The first buildings rose soon after the beginning of the year. Young Sutter's firm, Hensley, Reading & Co., probably erected the first frame building in the city.[65] This is disputed, however, by Pierre B. Cornwall, who claims the honor for himself, Albert Priest, and Barton Lee, in February, 1849.[66] J. Horace Culver states that the first building was erected at Front and J Streets by Sam Brannan as early as January 1, and that it was followed by those of Hensley and Reading at Front and I Streets and Priest, Lee & Co. at Second and J.[67]

63 *Calif. Star & Californian*, Dec. 16 and 23, 1848.
64 Burnett, *Recollections*, p. 294; Reed, *Hist. Sacramento County*, p. 61.
65 Colville, *Sacramento Directory, 1853–54*, p. 2, Bancroft, *Calif.*, VI, 448.
66 *Placer Times*, Dec. 15, 1849.
67 Culver, *Sacramento City Directory, 1851*, p. 72.

In the middle of 1848, after the gold discovery, McDougal & Co. tied up at the *Embarcadero* an old hulk loaded with merchandise from San Francisco, and thus became the first firm to do business on the site of Sacramento City. In August, George McDougal and his partners leased from Captain Sutter the rights to his ferry across the Sacramento. When he learned that a new city was planned, Mc-Dougal promptly claimed the exclusive use of a four-hundred-yard stretch of waterfront running south from the slough, as part of his leased rights to *exclusive trade at that point*. The southern bank of the slough was then just a little north of I Street. Young Sutter, having already bound himself to give one thousand yards to Hensley, Reading & Co., and later to the city *for her own use and benefit*, immediately rejected this false claim, leaving McDougal enraged and vengeful.[68]

Captain Sutter was still in the mountains when word of his son's town-building activity reached him. So enraged was he at this blow to his cherished hopes for Sutterville that he never forgave August, and a new and lasting chill settled upon their already cooling affection. *Had I not been snowed in at Coloma,* the senior Sutter told Hubert Howe Bancroft years later, *Sacramento never, never, would have been built.*[69]

Still fuming over their defeat, George McDougal and his associate, George McKinstry, hurried off to Coloma, where they first visited Lansford W. Hastings and quietly purchased from him a number of Sutterville lots, part of a half square mile he had acquired from Sutter, Sr., in 1845. Then they descended upon Sutter and, pointing out that they, too, were injured Sutterville landowners, enlarged upon the son's heinous crime of founding the rival Sacramento City until the old man's anger was whipped into a raging fury against his meddling child. Down from the mountains stormed the old pioneer in company with his deceivers. He refused to see August or Burnett

---

68 Bancroft, *Calif.,* VI, 448; Colville, *Sacramento Directory, 1853–54,* p. 2; *Placer Times,* June 28, 1850, reprinted *Sacramento Union,* Feb. 23, 1858; McChristian, *Narrative,* ms.; "H" to *Daily Herald,* Feb. 9, 1853; Sutter-McDougal agreement, Mar. 6, 1849, in Sutter Collection; Sutter, Jr., *Statement.*

69 Bancroft, *Calif.,* VI, 447; "H" to *Daily Herald,* Feb 9, 1853; Zollinger, *Sutter,* pp. 276–278.

and did not even stop at the Fort, but hurried on to San Francisco with McDougal, McKinstry, and Hastings.[70]

There these friends kept the wine bottle moving—in Sutter's direction—until, on March 6, he was induced to sign an infamous document which struck directly at his son's energetic efforts to rehabilitate the Sutter fortune by means of the new city. To compensate McDougal for the alleged loss of exclusive trading privileges at the *Embarcadero,* Sutter agreed to give him, within twenty days, title to a half square mile tract of land fronting 880 yards along the river and adjoining the southern edge of the Sutterville plat. For security, he promised that he *or the person in whom the legal title is nominally vested* would be bound *in the penal sum of Twenty Thousand Dollars for the faithful performance of this agreement within the time specified.*[71] That penalty forced young Sutter to fulfill the shameful agreement.

Confident that the time was now ripe to deliver the finishing blow to the young upstart of Sacramento City, George McDougal pulled his hulk and ferry away from the *Embarcadero* and withdrew with them to Sutterville.[72] Then, turning the fortunes of the firm over to his equally energetic brother John, recently arrived overland from Indiana, he left on a trip to the eastern states.[73] John immediately began a loud boosting of the old town hoping that it would soon eclipse the new community. Since Sacramento's chief advantage was its well known landing place, the *Embarcadero,* the new manager made every effort to set up a rival terminus for the San Francisco river boats. *The brigantine* Hope *will commence her regular trips between this place* [San Francisco] *and Suttersville, today,* advertised

[70] Sutter, Jr., *Statement*; Zollinger, *Sutter*, pp. 276–277.

[71] Sutter-McDougal agreement, Mar. 6, 1849, in Sutter Collection; Zollinger, *Sutter*, p. 276; Sutter, Jr., *Statement.* As recorded, the land joined the McKinstry property on the *north* side of Sutterville. The deed was dated June 19, well outside the 20-day limit, indicating that young Sutter held out as long as he could. (Sacramento County, *Deed Books*, vol. A, pp. 116–117.) Sutter, Jr., erroneously states that the land comprised one square mile and that the bond was for $40,000.

[72] Sutter, Testimony, *Placer Times,* June 28, 1850, reprinted in *Sacramento Union,* Feb. 23, 1858.

[73] Colville, *Sacramento Directory, 1853–54,* p. 2; Bancroft, *Calif.,* IV, 723; *Sacramento Union,* June 3, 1868.

Kybur & Stevens in March,[74] and McDougal at the same time ambitiously announced that the steamboat *J. A. Sutter* also would begin that run on the first of July.[75]

John, with a technique quite as adept as that of his brother George, next turned his attention to the leading Sacramento business houses. In March he offered several of these firms, including Sam Brannan, Hensley, Reading & Co., and Priest, Lee & Co., two hundred town lots each, provided that they remove their business and influence to Sutterville. Young Sutter had to meet this crisis without the wise counsel of Burnett, who had gone to San Francisco to meet the flood of incoming '49ers and push the interests of Sacramento City.[76] Faced with the threatened loss of his leading merchants, August saw only one alternative. He matched McDougal's offer by giving away lots in Sacramento City.[77]

McDougal's plot may also have affected the young Swiss in another way. The evident willingness of the other members of Hensley, Reading & Co. to profit by the offer most likely sowed discord in the firm, for August got out of it soon after. The withdrawal occurred on May 6, when he sold his interest in the business for four thousand dollars, half in gold at sixteen dollars an ounce and the remainder in goods.[78] Hensley, Reading & Co. continued in business until February 10, 1850, when the firm was dissolved and several of the members went into various banking concerns.[79]

McDougal next directed his attention to the numerous teamsters freighting goods from Sacramento to the mines, and tried to lure them to Sutterville with cut-rate prices. *CHEAPER THAN EVER,* he headed a mid-May advertisement in Sacramento's newborn newspaper:

[74] *Alta Calif.*, Mar. 22, 1849.

[75] *Ibid.*

[76] Burnett, *Recollections*, p. 299.

[77] Sutter, Jr., *Statement*; Dr. John Morse, in his historical sketch of Sacramento in Colville's *Directory* (p. 3), says that each of these merchants was offered 80 lots by McDougal, and that they managed to extort 500 lots from Sutter, Jr. This account is repeated in Bancroft, *Calif.*, VI, 448.

[78] Sacramento County, *Deed Books*, vol. A, p. 41.

[79] *Placer Times*, Mar. 2, 1850, quoted in Boggs, *My Playhouse*, p. 45.

We are now receiving 5200 bags superior flour, $16.00 per bag of 200 lbs. Our facilities will shortly enable us to sell this article at from 10 to $12.00. All other goods in proportion.[80]

This, and other attractive offers announced on huge placards, did not go unnoticed by the alert Sacramento traders. Fear of losing their lucrative trade with the freighters quickly drew them together and produced an astute retaliatory measure. Quietly combining forces, they made shrewd purchases of important goods from the cut-rate Sutterville merchant, who, by the time he knew what was happening, found many indispensable lines of his stock broken up. Since it often required considerable time to replenish certain goods, the attempted coup was neatly thwarted.[81]

John McDougal and George McKinstry were finding other difficulties in their camp. Hastings had turned out to be a vexing partner. He sold them only the lots at the two ends of the town, cautiously retaining the more valuable central area. Now he stubbornly refused to cooperate with his partners and sell his choice property at figures commensurate with the bargain prices they were asking for their less desirable lots. *The parties disagreed, and finally fell out altogether. Before the breach could be repaired, Sacramento had made such rapid strides that she could afford to laugh at her rival,* recalls an anonymous writer several years later.[82]

It soon became evident that the McDougals had finally been bested, for despite all their efforts Sutterville slowly declined, while the rival city was roaring with rapid growth. Thousands of gold seekers were making Sacramento City their outfitting point. Scores of little river schooners, brigs, and sloops, ignoring Sutterville's isolated highlands, were dumping mountains of supplies at the more convenient *Embarcadero* for freighting to the new mining camps. Besides its numerous merchant houses, Sacramento City had a newspaper, bakery, hotel, blacksmith-shop, pool hall, bowling alley, the

---

[80] *Placer Times,* May 19, 1849.
[81] Colville, *Sacramento Directory, 1853–54,* pp. 2–3; Bancroft, *Calif.,* VI, 450.
[82] "H" to *Daily Herald,* Feb. 9, 1853.

inevitable assortment of saloons, gambling houses, and brothels, and all the other appurtenances of a roaring frontier supply town.[83] The Fort was almost a deserted suburb, and as early as the middle of April the stores of Captain Dring and of Hensley, Reading & Co. were advertised to be *sold very low.*[84]

In spite of its low-lying, unhealthful site,[85] the new city had become by the summer of 1849 the unchallenged entrepôt of the northern mines. *Sacramento City is quite a flourishing place of some 300 Canvass Houses,* wrote one '49er on August 7; *building lots are from 600$ to 20,000.*[86] On August 2, when the French consul from Monterey passed northward, Sutterville *had only a score of buildings, forty to fifty tents and 400 to 500 inhabitants. Only six vessels, of from fifty to two hundred tons, were anchored in the port.*[87] And Bayard Taylor in October contrasted the Sutterville of *some thirty houses, scattered along the bank for half a mile,* with the *forest of masts along the embarcadero* at Sacramento.[88]

The quartering of some three hundred soldiers at Sutterville during the summer of 1849 delayed for only a brief moment the collapse of McDougal's grandiose schemes, and except for a short flurry in 1853, the town was never again able to challenge its rival.[89] In 1853, *Job,* a Sacramento newspaper correspondent, wrote: *In July, 1849, there was more capital interested in the prosperity of Sutterville, more shipping laying at her levee and the most formidable opposition ever known waged against us [Sacramento] . . . yet in three months this famous rival had but three old hulks at its bank, a few houses with goods that were eventually sold at auction, where they had be-*

---

[83] Bancroft, *Calif.,* VI, 449.

[84] *Alta Calif.,* Apr. 14, 1849, quoted in Boggs, *My Playhouse,* p. 26.

[85] " . . . from the quantity of Stagnet Water lying under the houses & holes in the streets there is really a very Bad smell thro' the town, and . . . it will lead to pestilence," wrote a visitor on May 28, 1850. (Thomas Kerr, "An Irishman in the Gold Rush," *Calif. Hist. Soc. Quarterly,* VIII [1929], 22.)

[86] Joseph L. Moody to his father, Aug. 7, 1849, in *Calif. Hist. Soc. Quarterly,* XIII (1934), 84–85.

[87] J. A. Moerenhout to the French Minister of Foreign Affairs, Sept. 1, 1849, in *Calif. Hist. Soc. Quarterly,* XIII (1934), 371.

[88] His *Eldorado,* I, 219.

[89] Bancroft, *Calif.,* VI, 450; George H. Baker, "Records of a California Residence," Soc. Calif. Pioneers, *Quarterly,* VIII (1931), 44.

come nearly worthless, presenting a perfect picture of a deserted village.[90]

The tremendous sale of lots in Sacramento City at last removed from Captain Sutter's shoulders the great debts he had contracted in the years preceding the gold rush. Even the largest of these, that to the Russian American Fur Company, now pared down to approximately twenty thousand dollars, was at last paid in full. Burnett reports that shortly after he had taken charge of young Sutter's affairs, Colonel William M. Steuart arrived from San Francisco, announced himself as the company's attorney, and demanded payment of the balance of the seven-year-old debt incurred by the purchase of Fort Ross and Bodega. Steuart was insistent and ready to attach the vast Sutter estate to assure payment. Burnett immediately sensed the danger, for such an attachment would have been followed immediately by that of every other creditor. This would have enjoined the sale of lots, the Sutters' only source of income, and involved the estate in a tangle of litigation, which might have resulted in a total loss for all parties. He was cautious enough, however, to demand that Steuart show the actual contract between Sutter and the Russians as proof of his power to collect for the company. Burnett writes: *I assured him that our intentions were to pay the Company as early as possible, and I gave him my personal pledge that I would myself see that the debt to the Company should be secured by the assignment to the Company of good notes, so soon as he should produce the original contract.*

Without this personal pledge I think he would have at once commenced an action to subject the property of the estate to the debt due the Company and that his affidavit that he was the attorney of the plaintiff would have been held as sufficient by the court. Under all the circumstances I think I have a just right to claim that I saved the estate from great embarrassment if not from final ruin.

On the 13th of April 1849, in the city of San Francisco, I paid to Col. Steuart $800 in gold and assigned to him $18,988 in notes, making the sum total of $19,788, he having, in the mean time received

---

[90] *Alta Calif.*, Feb. 4, 1853.

the contract from the Company.[91] This statement by Burnett is significant, since it is perhaps the first definite detailed proof that the Sutter debt to the Russians was finally paid.

Despite his extravagant inefficiency in the management of New Helvetia, the elder Sutter was unhappy to have his business affairs in the hands of others, even a son and a trusted agent who were paying off one by one a stack of old debts he himself could never have surmounted. Chafing and restless, his dissatisfaction constantly fanned by dubious friends who had reason to dislike the efficient new managers, he was impatient to get the estate back into his own hands.

The son, still less than a year in California, had experienced since his arrival nothing but a series of troubles. Despite his energy in developing Sacramento City, so that by the middle of August his father's enormous debts were paid,[92] the young man's presence was still resented. Never was this son able to find the affectionate father he had a right to expect. Lienhard recalls that sometime in 1849 he reprimanded the old man for threatening his own flesh and blood. Blinded by insane passion, the father snatched up a heavy double-barreled pistol, ready to shoot himself. Lienhard wrenched the weapon from his hand. Though the pistol was not loaded, the elder Sutter's action showed the great intensity of his feeling.[93]

The young man's *Statement*, wherein these troubles form but the prelude to further trials, contains the unhappy record of his father's dislike and of his continued injustice to him. Between words of deep despair, flashes of unrestrained and justified passion fire each page. By 1855, when he put the facts to paper, he had experienced much of the cruelty and ugliness of that early period in California history. His account forms a valuable contemporary picture of unscrupulous business dealings. Perhaps, because this revealing manuscript has remained almost unknown since the rampant times it depicts so well, the very men who bilked its author so thoroughly and shamelessly— notably Sam Brannan and Julius Wetzlar—have been remembered

[91] Burnett to Sutter, Jr., Jan. 18, 1894, in Sutter, Jr., papers. See also Bancroft, *Calif.*, IV, 189; Zollinger, *Sutter*, p. 275.

[92] Burnett, *Recollections*, p. 288; Sutter, Jr., *Statement*.

[93] Lienhard, *Pioneer*, pp. 207–208.

by a lenient posterity as business men of enterprise and propriety.

August's reminiscences show clearly that the Sutters were both poor businessmen.[94] The utter faith which they placed in their associates was positively naive. Often they secured not even the slightest guarantee before entrusting valuable properties to the itching fingers of almost complete strangers.[95] Though it is questionable whether the most astute—and honest—agent could have kept the original Sutter domain intact, August believed that if the business-like Burnett had been retained, his father would have become one of the richest men in California. But the times were too hectic for ordinary dealings, and men were feverish with the urge to make big money in a short time. Speculation quickly overran the bounds of prudence, the unsettled status of the law and its controllable machinery were an open invitation to corruption, and the existence of vast holdings without definite boundary lines was an irresistible lure to land-grabbing, money-hungry men. What the Sutters could have salvaged had they adopted the morals and methods of the time will ever remain an interesting conjecture.

By June 15, 1849, all the old debts had been paid except the one to Antonio Suñol, and August, ill at Hock Farm and weak with fever, returned the property to his father. He held out only a half square mile of land adjoining the northern boundary of Sutterville and four days later deeded this to George McDougal. Thus he complied with the fraudulent agreement coaxed out of his wine-befuddled father on March 6.[96] After the transfer, August remained in retirement at Hock Farm, apparently inactive and unwell most of the time.

Archibald Peachy and Henry A. Schoolcraft, who were to replace Burnett as Sutter agents in San Francisco and Sacramento, were both at Hock Farm and witnessed the transfer. Neither they nor the

---

[94] Once when Sutter, Jr., entrusted Lienhard with a large amount of gold, Lienhard offered to give him a receipt. "Why a receipt?" asked August. "If you are honest, everything will be all right, if you are not, a receipt is of no value." (Lienhard, *Pioneer,* p. 208.)

[95] See Sutter, Jr., *Statement.*

[96] Sacramento County, *Deed Books,* vol. A, pp. 69–70, 116–117.

Sutters notified Burnett at the time; August was ill in bed, and his father was merely negligent. Burnett continued to sell lots under the old agreement for some time before he received word that he was no longer agent for the Sutter property.

Burnett was now beginning to develop political aspirations and may not have been averse to relinquishing the agency. Still he was not going to be sloughed off without something to show for it. By the terms of the original agreement *said John A. Sutter, Jr. stipulated on his part to place all the town property in Sacramento city in the hands of said Burnett for sale.*[97] Burnett's commission was one-fourth of the gross proceeds, and he now sought compensation from the elder Sutter for his share of the unsold lots. On July 24 they agreed that Burnett was to close all sales he had made before the notification, that he was to advance $10,000 for payment of the long-standing Suñol debt (to be repaid from Sutter's portion of notes as they were collected) and in return was to receive *certain town lots* in Sacramento. It might seem that Sutter for once got the better of a business deal. The *certain town lots,* however, amounted to no less than eighty-two square city blocks plus an additional 109 lots in various parts of the city.[98] Captain Sutter, who long before had taken a great dislike to Burnett as his son's agent, once snapped years later that Burnett *made a fortune much too quickly to suit me.*[99]

About March young Sutter had begun to send livestock and household effects up from the Fort in order to make Hock Farm more comfortable for his father and for the family when they could be brought from Switzerland. His father's excesses and the thought of his mother and the children in Switzerland were a constant worry to him. His father made no effort to effect a reunion with the family, and at last August took the matter into his own hands and asked Heinrich Lienhard to act as his agent in bringing them to California. Lienhard agreed to do this for $4000 plus about $8000 travelling expenses, part of which August found it necessary to borrow from

---

[97] Sacramento County, *Deed Books,* vol. C, p. 250.
[98] *Ibid.,* vol. C, p. 250–255.
[99] Gudde, *Sutter's Own Story,* p. 222.

William Daylor, the owner of a ranch and trading post on the Cosumnes River.[100]

On June 20, while young Sutter was ill at Hock Farm, Lienhard left San Francisco on the steamer *Panama* for Europe via the Isthmus. He returned on the same ship, with Mrs. Sutter, Emil, Alphonse, and Eliza, as well as a number of relatives of the Sutters, reaching San Francisco on January 21, 1850. After installing his charges in a hotel he took a river steamer to Sacramento, where he met Captain Sutter and informed him of the safe arrival of his long-deserted family. The two of them hurried back to San Francisco without notifying August, who was still at Hock. Lienhard states that he thought the elder Sutter had taken steps to send his son the news, but the father was too excited or, more likely, wanted to see Frau Sutter before August could talk, and consequently no message was sent to him. This omission resulted in some coolness between August and Lienhard.[101]

A reporter, confident that the elder Sutter must have been delighted with the arrival of his family, pencilled this ungrammatical euphuism:

A Joyous Meeting—*The veteran pioneer, Captain Sutter, will welcome to his adopted home, his family and numerous friends of early years, who are among the passengers by the last steamer. After an absence from "faderland" of nearly twenty years, which period has been fraught with event in the wilds of California, we can readily imagine the happiness with which the distinguished adventurer will greet familiar forms and faces, endeared by the sacred ties of relationship, to the country which he has learned to love so well. Twenty years' separation from family and friends is indeed a blank in one's existence when eked out in the wilderness.*[102]

The Sutter family proceeded to their new home at Hock, and shortly afterwards Lienhard arrived to visit and to settle his account with young Sutter. August's illness and long inactivity had evidently

---

[100] Lienhard, *Pioneer*, pp. 192–194; Davis, *Illus. Hist. Sacramento County*, p. 235.

[101] Lienhard, *Californien*, pp. 288–290.

[102] *Alta Calif.*, Jan. 24, 1850.

effected quite a change in him. When Lienhard stepped off the steamer at Hock he noticed *an unfamiliar figure clad in buckskin trousers and a red flannel shirt. He had a brown felt hat on his head, and was wearing a long bowie knife in a leather belt around his waist. He walked slowly from the house down to the river. Thirty or forty feet away he stopped and looked, first at me, and then off across the river. He seemed to be a stranger, so I did not pay any attention to him. . . . In a short time old Captain Sutter, cane in hand, appeared. He stopped near the man I had taken for a stranger, and after we had greeted one another, I asked where his son, August, was, as he had not appeared. Sutter pointed to the man, who resembled a disreputable gold miner, and said: "My August? Why there he is!"*[103]

"*He your son?*" *I said, looking incredulous. I hardly knew whether I had heard him right, but Sutter said, smiling a little, yes, he was the same. I came a little closer to the two men in order to get a better look at the younger one. Because I thought he might be jesting a little at my expense I meant to address him in a friendly manner. But I noticed such a gloomy expression on his face that my friendly words remained unspoken. He did not offer his hand to welcome me, nor did he say a kind word, but just stared at me with his big, light grey, nearsighted eyes, so that I hardly knew what to make of it all and almost wished I were carrying a revolver, or at least a bowie knife as big as the one he was carrying. I could not think of anything I had done to justify such a reception, and I thought that I had fulfilled all my duties during the journey. I think I now became a little reticent myself in spite of the friendly words of the elder Sutter. . . . I knew that I must somehow have given cause for the young man's unfriendly behavior. Perhaps I had hurt his feelings by not asking him to meet his family in San Francisco, because, after all, it was he, and not his father, who had sent me to Switzerland after them. If he had been in Sacramento when I informed his father of our arrival, I should have notified him, too, and left it up to them which one should come to San Francisco to meet the family.*

---

[103] Lienhard, *Pioneer*, p. 226. The remainder of this incident, omitted from the book, is taken from a photostat of folio 199 of the original manuscript, furnished by Mrs. E. J. Magnuson. The translation is by Mrs. Grete Frugé.

Puzzling over August's deliberate coolness, Lienhard recalled that he had written him only two letters during his absence. *Perhaps I should have written a half dozen. Moreover, there was a question whether he had even seen these letters,* he wrote, revealing a glimpse of the bitter feelings between father and son. *But even if I admitted being somewhat in the wrong his unfriendly and even repulsive behavior hardly seemed justified. I would have accepted an expression of criticism, although he could hardly have had anything else against me. But such a reception was really insulting.*

In spite of that I intended to stay at Hock Farm the next few days, but young Mr. August seemed bent on annoying me a little more. I felt that all the more in the evening when the young gentleman sought every opportunity to prove to me that I was not a welcome guest. I now expressed my dissatisfaction openly in the presence of his younger brothers and remarked that I had neither deserved nor expected such treatment, and that I did not at all intend to be in anybody's way here but would look for shelter elsewhere the following day. My words were at once reported to the parents.

Lienhard had now worked himself into such a state of resentment that he walked out of the house, wrapped himself in his blankets and was preparing to sleep outdoors, when Mrs. Sutter appeared and soothed his ruffled feelings sufficiently to get him back inside.

I had already wrapped myself in my blankets again, he goes on, *and had lain down on the floor next to some other sleepers when the stern young gentleman appeared and asked in a loud voice where I was. I soon showed him by my loud answer where I could be found. He said:*

"Mr. Lienhard, I want to settle with you."

"That's quite all right with me," I told him; "that can be done soon enough."

I named the sum which I had spent for the family in recent weeks from my own pocket and then remarked, by the way, that I had not made a specific list of expenses for everything else. I said that at the beginning of the trip I had intended to keep such a list, but that Mrs. Sutter had not thought it necessary, and I had not done it. The stern young man seemed satisfied and promised to reimburse me the next day. After that I would have spent the first night without further disturbance if it had not been for the many fleas.[104]

The next day Lienhard received his money from August, and since *the young man was not so grouchy today,* and the old folks insisted that he consider himself at home, he changed his mind and remained a few days longer. It seems clear that August was under severe mental strain, for Lienhard declares that after he came back with the family he heard that *the captain's son, August, was drinking and had developed a taste for whiskey.*[105]

Once the family was installed at Hock Farm, Captain Sutter felt that his son was in the way, probably because he knew too much about his father's personal life. Sutter suggested that August go into business somewhere and promised him $30,000 capital to get started. Accepting the suggestion, August then began a second period of unhappy business relations with sharper men than he.

Through Dr. C. Brandes, a German physician who attended him at Hock, August met the brothers Gustavus and Julius Wetzlar, a pair of lace merchants from Leipzig, who had established a general trading house at Sacramento and Auburn. The Wetzlars were attracted by the elder Sutter's offer of capital and they persuaded the son, still ill and not very enthusiastic, to enter into a partnership with them and Brandes. The troubles that immediately beset him are described in great detail in his *Statement.*

By the terms of the partnership August was bound to bring $30,000 into the business. He never received the money from his father and was soon forced to borrow all he could from his mother and even

---

[104] Lienhard was certainly in no mood to renew his acquaintance with this curse of early day California. Walter Colton, a navy chaplain and *alcalde* at Monterey, wrote in 1846: "The trouble of young and old here is the flea. The native who is thoroughly inured to his habits may little heed him, but he keeps the stranger in a constant nettle. One would suppose, from his indiscriminate and unmitigated hostility, he considered himself the proprietor of all California." (Colton, *Three Years in Calif.,* p. 70.)

[105] Lienhard, *Pioneer,* p. 233. In his later life August was said to be an abstainer. It is interesting to note, however, that at a party for his daughter Cristina, on her fifteenth birthday, two drinks made him so violently ill that the girl was embarrassed before her guests. (Statement by Mrs. Anna Sutter Young.)

from his sister's beau;[106] he also sold a number of horses and mules that remained in his possession. His partners continued to press him and urged him to intervene in his father's affairs to prevent, as they said, the loss of the family property. Finally, with Dr. Brandes, he went to Hock Farm and confronted his father. After a stormy scene, Captain Sutter on May 7, 1850, *for One Dollar, good and lawful money of the United States of America,* deeded to his son all his lots and buildings in Sacramento,[107] and on May 11, for another dollar, he transferred a half square mile of land lying between Sacramento and Sutterville.[108]

The transfer benefited August very little and was an immediate cause of worry to him. Free soilers squatted on choice lots and defied the owners to oust them; taxes for extensive levees to protect the town against a recurrence of the flood of 1849–50 promised to be high; double sales of lots made by the elder Sutter and his two agents resulted in constant confusion, adjustment, and uncertainty.

It was too much for August, who was ill and tired. Perhaps he could sell and get out. He confided as much to Julius Wetzlar one day, and that wily merchant pricked up his ears. It would be difficult, he said, to find buyers for so large a property, but he would exert himself in the matter. So well did he exert himself, going quietly among his friends, that only a few days elapsed before he had a formidable group of buyers lined up. A quartet, headed by Sam Brannan and including Samuel Bruce, James H. Grahame, and Julius Wetzlar, offered August $125,000 for his entire property as it stood, agreeing to pay taxes for that year, to assume the expense of any title suits, and to fight the increasingly troublesome squatters. Besides the Sacramento property, described briefly as *consisting of two thousand two hundred (2200) town lots, be the same more or less, said lots being bounded according to the original plat or plan of said city,* there were included five shares in the town of Eliza, lots in the other paper towns of Plumas and Nicolaus, a lot in San Francisco, and the half square mile of land

---

106 Lienhard, *Pioneer,* pp. 245–246.

107 Sacramento County, *Deed Books,* vol. C, p. 224.

108 *Ibid.,* pp. 223–224.

between Sacramento and Sutterville.[109] August now had to make a fateful decision and he chose to sell.

William Mesick, who fought a long court battle over the property a few years later, charged that Wetzlar and Brandes conspired to cheat young Sutter. According to Mesick, Sutter was too ill to leave his room and asked to have the papers brought to him. Wetzlar refused and Brandes administered a powerful medicine which enabled Sutter to accompany them to the lawyer's office. There for the first time August learned that Wetzlar, whom he had supposed to be only his agent, was also one of the buyers. The terms of the deed were not what he expected and at first August refused to sign. Thereupon Wetzlar told him that his life depended on his getting out of the state to a more healthful climate, and finally, in full weariness, he accepted the terms.[110]

The following public announcement appeared in the press[111] on June 22:

> NOTICE is hereby given that I have authorized and fully empowered Sam'l Brannan, Samuel C. Bruce, Julius Wetzlar and James S. Graham to sell, dispose of, and convey all lands, tenements, hereditaments and real estate whatever, in the state of California, to, or in which I am or may be interested. And also, in my name, to sue for and collect all sum or sums of money that is now or may hereafter become due me, for the sale of real estate in the state of California.   JOHN A. SUTTER, JR.
> Witnessed by Benj. Fenner and Walter R. Smith.
> sacramento city, June 21st, 1850.

An initial installment of $25,000 was to be paid to Sutter, Jr., before July 1, a like sum three months later, and the final $75,000 a year from the date of the sale. What the record calls a *deed condi-*

---

[109] Sacramento County, *Deed Books,* vol. D, pp. 191–194.

[110] *Brannan* v. *Mesick,* in 6th Judicial Dist. Court (Sacramento), *Cases,* 2nd ser., nos. 2985, 3909 (1855).

[111] It ran in the *Sacramento Transcript* for one month beginning June 22, 1850.

tional was made and filed on June 20, 1850, and on the following day payment of the first installment was acknowledged.[112] Even this first obligation was not fully met. Wetzlar postponed payment of his share to Sutter and topped it off by borrowing another two thousand dollars from him. The final pages of the *Statement,* an account of young Sutter's futile efforts to collect the other installments, show how he was slowly ruined by the sale.

Immediately following the transaction, Bruce disposed of one half of his quarter share to W. D. M. Howard for $18,625.[113] On July 10, Grahame sold half of his quarter to Warbass, Heyle, & Morse, the Sacramento bankers, for $25,625,[114] and on February 28, 1851, Brannan certified that he held his share in trust for the equal benefit of himself and Theodore Shillaber.[115] Only Wetzlar hung on to his full quarter share.

For a time August felt confident of the future. In the deed conditional he had appointed Wetzlar his agent to collect the later installments, and he was now determined to leave California. Rising from his sick bed, he made a hurried trip to Hock Farm to take leave of his mother. Although he had no definite plans, he secured letters of introduction to persons in Lima, Guayaquil, and other cities and booked passage on the mail steamer leaving the first of July.

Just before he left Hock Farm for San Francisco, a strange story appeared in the *Alta California,* written by that paper's Sacramento correspondent.

A singular spectacle is said to have occurred at Hock Farm a few evenings since, in which the son of Capt. J. A. Sutter signalised himself by setting fire to the Indian Ranchoria of that place, and creating an alarm which was only allayed by the interference of strangers on the spot. The only reason assigned for this strange behavior is that the young man conceived that an indignity had been put upon him by the Indians attached to the Farm. He is now in this city [Sacramento].[116]

---

[112] Sacramento County, *Deed Books,* vol. D, p. 195.
[113] *Ibid.,* vol. E, pp. 274–276.
[114] *Ibid.,* vol. D, p. 274.
[115] *Ibid.,* vol. G, p. 23.
[116] *Alta Calif.,* June 26, 1850. It is possible that this story may have referred to Emil or Alphonse, but usually "the son" meant August, the eldest.

It is difficult to judge whether this was a true story or merely an attempt to smear his character. If true, it shows how far trouble, illness and drugs had sapped his nervous strength.

On July 1, 1850, John August Sutter, Jr., accompanied by his physician, the double-tongued Dr. Brandes, boarded the Pacific Mail Steamship Company's pioneer steamer *California*.[117] Leaving behind him two years of intense disappointment and worry, he passed through the Golden Gate on his way to Panama, and turned his eyes southward in search of health and a new life.

He got no farther than Acapulco. Forsaking Dr. Brandes, who continued toward the eastern states, August remained in the sunny little Mexican port where he found the haven he had been seeking. Here in new surroundings were happiness and peace and a refreshed outlook on life. He had hardly discovered Acapulco when what he writes of nebulously as *an other important incident of my life* definitely decided him to adopt the little adobe town as his home. Undoubtedly the important incident was his meeting with Señorita Maria del Carmen Rivas, a young woman described as *extremely pleasant and amiable and the most elegant in the city of Acapulco*. She was the daughter of Francisco and Dorotea Camano de Rivas, highly respected citizens who, because of their Spanish blood, were said to have been cruelly treated by Don Juan Alvarez, the famed Indian nationalist patriot and governor of Guerrero. As a consequence of this persecution, Señorita Maria's parents, with their four sons and four daughters, were living quietly and in reduced circumstances.[118]

Once free of the enervating influence of Dr. Brandes, August suddenly bloomed in the light of Maria's dark eyes and captivating smile. The sick, weary boy of Sacramento became the warm-worded suitor of the charming señorita, and in the latter part of 1850, within a few months after his arrival, they were married in the parish church of Acapulco.[119]

But August did not spend all his time in courting. In Acapulco he

---

[117] *Alta Calif.*, July 1 and 2, 1850.
[118] Hull to the writer, Feb. 21, 1941. Hull quotes largely from a letter dictated to his mother's cousin by his grandaunt.
[119] *Ibid.*

met Julius Lecacheux, a Frenchman from San Francisco, who had recently brought down a vessel freighted with goods for the Mexican market. Lecacheux was the senior member of the firm of J. Lecacheux & L. Galley, wine merchants at 54 Merchant Street,[120] and he offered to August an interest in the Mexican branch of his business. The young Swiss promptly accepted and took charge of the Acapulco office. When the Frenchman returned to California he carried young Sutter's power of attorney and tried to collect from Wetzlar the second installment of $25,000. When he was rudely ignored he sent his new partner an urgent appeal to come to San Francisco at once. August's worries were renewed; leaving his bride of but a few weeks, he boarded the first steamer touching at Acapulco, the *Tennessee,* and arrived at San Francisco January 8, 1851.[121]

The second installment of $25,000 was more than three months overdue. The Brannan-Bruce-Grahame-Wetzlar combine complained that they did not get all they had bargained for, and they made no effort to pay or to reach a new settlement. The property deeded to them included a half square mile of river frontage between Sacramento and Sutterville, a piece which August received from his father on May 11. But just five days earlier Captain Sutter had sold a two-thirds interest in the entire river front between the two cities to Dr. Thomas J. White and Cadwalader Ringgold.[122] The four buyers insisted that they had been unable to take possession of this property, on which they placed the disproportionate value of $40,000, and claimed a deduction of that sum from the purchase price. August evidently had not known of the double sale. He replied that they had offered $125,000 for his property as it stood, had agreed to fight any legal battles for clear titles, knowing that they might expect difficulties from squatters and double sales, and had agreed to make no further claims on him.[123] The Brannan group sat tight and awaited developments.

It was Sutter, Jr., who took the first action. With no papers, guar-

[120] Parker, *San Francisco Directory, 1852–53.*
[121] *Alta Calif.,* Jan. 9, 1851.
[122] Sacramento County, *Deed Books,* vol. D, p. 134.
[123] Sutter, Jr., *Statement.*

antees, or mortgages to safeguard the deed conditional, he realized that he was in a difficult position and ranged against formidable opponents. He retained the services of the prominent San Francisco law firm, Burritt, Yale & Musson, at a fee of one-fourth of any moneys realized. After a study of the situation, the lawyers suddenly lost interest, and their unhurried manner in the case soon began to tell on August's nerves. The date for the final payment approached with still no sign of the second installment.

There are many conflicting statements about that second installment, but the evidence seems to indicate that it was considered covered in a final compromise settlement reached later. Young Sutter makes no mention of any earlier payment in the *Statement*. A. Wardwell, the notary public who executed the papers of the final settlement, declared in a deposition to the court: *There was a controversy between him* [Sutter, Jr.] *and the parties in relation to the payments—the second installment had become due and they refused to pay it, because they found that they did not get so much as they had bargained for.*[124] In the case of *Brannan* v. *Mesick et al* Julius Wetzlar testified that he had paid his share, but made no clear-cut statement about the others. The character of Wetzlar as portrayed by young Sutter, and the astonishingly convenient lack of memory he exhibited at several points during his lengthy cross-examination, do not incline one to place much confidence in his testimony. The fact that all his papers had burned in the great fire at Sacramento in November, 1852, probably gave him added assurance.

What was the general compromise settlement? The situation had reached an impasse when, according to August, Brannan approached him with an offer of $40,000, and he, despairing of ever getting his full payment, accepted the proposal. Wetzlar testified that August suggested the compromise. Wardwell, who was present during the final agreement, stated: *The parties and John A. Sutter Jr. talked the matter over together in my presence . . . and a compromise was made that the parties should pay him forty thousand dollars, and notes were executed. . . . John A. Sutter* [Jr.] *came several times to Mr. Brannan*

---

124 The deposition was taken Feb. 19, 1857, at San Francisco.

to get a settlement. The forty thousand dollars was intended as a pay-
ment of the $100,000 Dollars indebtedness. This deduction was made
on account of his inability to convey all the land he had agreed to,
and some other offset or claim which they had against him which I
cannot bring to mind what it was. This other claim was for $20,000
paid in taxes,[125] although Wetzlar glibly declared there was no such
deduction.

In this transaction, which took place on March 18, 1851, Sutter
received no actual cash, but notes due on July 1. Wetzlar testified
that either three or five thousand dollars cash was paid by Brannan,
Bruce, Grahame and himself in equal parts. Wardwell, who drew up
the papers, remembered no cash payments. To obtain the notes for
$40,000 August was forced to make out two receipts, one for the sec-
ond installment of $25,000, and another for the final payment of
$75,000[126]—moneys he never saw! And before he was able to collect
on the notes he was again set upon and victimized. So assailed was
he by court suits, injunctions, protests of notes and alleged inability
(or refusal) to pay, that he was able to salvage from the wreckage of
his once magnificent estate only a paltry $3,500—and he was $3,839
in debt!

Shortly after the March agreement the four buyers, together with
Dr. Thomas J. White and his partners, began juggling titles to the
land between Sacramento and Sutterville. White it was whose partial
title to the river front had given the Brannan group an excuse to deduct $40,000 from their debt to Sutter. Hundreds of acres changed
hands in a number of deals, solely for the legal fee of $10 per deal.[127]
The last of these transfers was concluded on June 26, and the next
day Brannan, Bruce, Grahame, and Wetzlar began slicing their melon.
To Brannan went 54 blocks and 125 lots in Sacramento, and 12
lots of ten acres each, *free of all encumbrances,* lying between Sacramento and Sutterville.[128] Bruce received 57½ blocks, 120 town lots,

[125] Sutter, Jr., *Statement.*
[126] Sacramento County, *Powers of Attorney,* vol. A, pp. 393–395; Sacramento
County, *Deed Books,* vol. 57, pp. 10–11.
[127] Sacramento County, *Deed Books,* vol. G, pp. 271–281.
[128] *Ibid.,* pp. 274–278.

and 12 of the ten-acre lots.[129] Grahame was apportioned 62½ blocks, 127 town lots, and 12 ten-acre lots.[130] Wetzlar's share was 58½ blocks, 124 town lots, and 11 ten-acre lots.[131]

Shortly afterwards Sutter, Jr., disappeared. In the spring of 1852 he turned up at Guaymas on the Mexican northwest coast where his eldest child, John Sutter III, was born.[132] Always a nervous man,[133] he was then under a tremendous mental strain. *I found myself,* he wrote, *through the connivance and miserable tricks of some designing men who probably now laughed at me in easy circumstances, always misunderstood by my father, even by my mother and my own brothers, with my reputation tarnished, represented everywhere as a man of loose, prodigal and intemperate habits who had squandered away his fortune, deserving nobody's help or support, with my body ruined by sickness and medicines, with a wife and child depending upon me and with poverty and misery staring to me in the face.*[134]

What he did in Guaymas is unknown, although he is said to have lost all his money there.[135] He did not remain long. Evidently in search of solitude and mental rest, he and his family soon penetrated deep into a wild wasteland in the state of Sonora. There among the Indians they experienced for two and a half years what he calls *incredible sufferings and mental agonies.* Further details of that curious interlude in his life he passes over with deliberate reticence, and the reader can only imagine such a life on the blazing desert, far from civilization.

Whatever the actual events of this strange sojourn, it was here in the wilderness sometime in 1854 that a letter from his younger brother Alphonse reached him. It was common rumor in Sacramento, Alphonse wrote, that Dr. Brandes had kept August under the influence of drugs and poisons, so benumbing his mind that the doctor and his accomplice Wetzlar could more easily deceive him. Several lawyers

---

[129] Sacramento County, *Deed Books,* vol. H, pp. 65–68.
[130] *Ibid.,* vol. G, pp. 290–293.
[131] *Ibid.,* pp. 268–271. The lots which were divided among the Brannan associates are listed also in *Sacramento Union,* Oct. 2, 1856.
[132] Hull to the writer, Feb. 21, 1941.
[133] Statement by Mrs. Young.
[134] Sutter, Jr., *Statement.*
[135] Hull to the writer, Feb. 21, 1941.

believed something could still be salvaged from the wreck of his fortune. The explanation came as a great light to August and drew him once more to California. Listed among the passengers of the steamer *Sierra Nevada,* arriving at San Francisco October 15, 1854, were *J Sutter wife and 2 children.*[136]

That Sutter, Jr., still hoped to recover at least part of his property is clear from the *Statement,* which was written at San Francisco, in February, 1855. He mentions no plan of action, and it is not known whether any definite steps were taken. He had in mind that the original transfer of New Helvetia from his father to him could be proved illegal, thus causing the entire property to revert to his father. This expectation must have been a forlorn hope indeed.

August and his wife visited the family at Hock Farm, and left little John III there to spend the rest of his childhood in the care of his grandparents. August again became run-down and ill. Less than a year after they arrived, the young Sutters went back to Mexico—to the one spot in which they had found happiness, Acapulco. There, in the city that was to remain his home for the rest of his life, August once more set about mending his fortunes.

Shortly thereafter he was visited by William S. Mesick, a former employee in the recorder's office in Sacramento County. Mesick, whose work with the records of property sales had made him familiar with young Sutter's deed conditional, found a ready listener to his plan for breaking the power of Brannan, Bruce, Grahame, and Wetzlar. On July 9, 1855, he secured from Sutter, Jr., a deed to the Sacramento property already made over to the Brannan group on June 20, 1850. This time, however, each block and lot was carefully enumerated.[137] It is not certain what terms were agreed upon, but Mesick seems to have paid Sutter several hundred dollars and given him a penal bond, perhaps to guarantee additional payment.[138]

[136] *Alta Calif.,* Oct. 16, 1854. This was in error, for John III was still their only child.

[137] Sacramento County, *Deed Books,* vol. P, pp. 427–432. A list was printed in the *Sacramento Union* Aug. 1, 1855, and reprinted Sept. 30, 1856. It included 236½ blocks, mostly in the east and south parts of the city, and 421½ lots.

[138] *Brannan v. Mesick,* in Labatt, *Reports,* I, 34.

Eager to test the validity of his new title, Mesick speedily returned to California, recorded his deed on July 30,[139] and instituted in the district court at Sacramento a suit to eject one Thomas Sunderland, an owner under the Brannan deed.[140] By this action Mesick pressed several attacks against the Brannan title. In the first place, he argued that the deed from Sutter, Jr., to Brannan and his associates was invalid for want of sufficient description of the property.[141] Furthermore, the contract provided that the title should not pass to Brannan and the others until payment of the purchase price was made, and Mesick held that proof of such payment devolved upon the purchasers. The recording of the deed, he claimed, did not of itself affect the rights of a subsequent buyer. Sunderland, in answer, claimed legal title to the property and maintained that Sutter, Jr., had no title to convey to Mesick. The trial was cut short when Sunderland, claiming insufficient evidence, entered a demurrer which was sustained by the court. Mesick appealed the case to the state Supreme Court.[142]

On September 30, 1856, Chief Justice Hugh C. Murray and Justice David S. Terry of the Supreme Court ruled that the lower court was in error in sustaining the demurrer. They recognized young Sutter's apparent intention to convey the property to the Brannan group, but placed equal importance on the nature of the deed, which withheld the title until payment had been made. Consequently the recording of such a deed was not a definite proof of title, and did not place upon Mesick the responsibility of inquiring into its validity. The demurrer was not sustained, and the case was remanded to the lower court for retrial.[143]

The Supreme Court had settled only a preliminary legal point, but real estate dealers and property owners were considerably worried, and the editor of the *Sacramento Union* viewed the action as a portent of things to come. *The decision,* he commented, *is couched in*

---

[139] Sacramento County, *Deed Books,* vol. P, p. 432.

[140] Sunderland held title to the block bounded by S, T, Ninth and Tenth Streets.

[141] Described only as "consisting of two thousand two hundred (2200) town lots, be the same more or less."

[142] *Mesick* v. *Sunderland,* in *Calif. Reports,* VI (1856), 297–298.

[143] *Ibid.,* pp. 297–316; reprinted in *Sacramento Union,* Sept. 30, 1856.

such language as to leave very little doubt what the conclusion of the court will finally be. . . .[144] *Possibly this may be good law, but if it is, it presents a case where law and justice are not united, where the administration of the law will work the rankest injustice. . . . It is the first really heavy blow that has been judicially struck against titles in this city, and will be felt accordingly. The decision fell like a clap of thunder in a clear sky upon most of our citizens. . . . Nearly, if not all, of this property was in the hands of parties who had bought and paid a full price for it, under the firm belief that the title was a legal one. If Mesick succeeds, these innocent purchasers must suffer heavily. If John A. Sutter, Jr., had been paid once for this property, and then sold it the second time, he must be a man lost to all sense of honor and honesty.*[145]

This last remark aroused General Sutter, living in retirement at Hock Farm, to rush to the defense of his son. *It seems that it is very little known,* he wrote to the *Union, that my son, J. A. Sutter, Jr., who sold his interest in this property to Bruce, Brannan & Co. for one hundred and twenty-five thousand dollars, has received not more than twelve or thirteen thousand dollars on account of this large sum, promised in 1850. Out of the remaining sum he has been swindled. It was in vain that he wrote to these men—he never could get a dollar more from them. Several years past my son took much trouble to employ some lawyers, on various occasions, in San Francisco and Sacramento. When he came here, once, he found one; but he was bought by this company, and would have nothing to do with this affair. Others refused their services to him because he was poor, and had no money to pay these heartless lawyers in advance; and another class of lawyers were afraid, or did not like to take up this case, against the millionaire, Sam Brannan, and his three associates in this affair.*

At last one had the courage to undertake this work. It was Wm. S. Mesick, who studied this transaction, through and through, and made a trip to Acapulco, to see Sutter, Jr.—made him propositions, which were accepted and agreed upon, and so the matter stands now; and,

---

[144] *Sacramento Union,* Sept. 30, 1856.
[145] *Ibid.,* Oct. 1, 1856.

thank God in heaven, the Courts in California are just in these days.[146]

This letter brought an immediate response from Wetzlar, who insisted that payments had been made from time to time, and that the final settlement had been entirely satisfactory to Sutter, Jr. Then, in a rapier thrust at one of the elder Sutter's weaknesses, he remarked: *It is well known that Gen. Sutter is very much in the habit of signing deeds, and other papers and instruments, without knowing what they contain. It is not necessary to notice the charge of swindling, which he has signed for somebody.*[147]

The next round in the legal contest was a clash between Brannan and Mesick. Before Judge Monson of the Sixth Judicial Court in the April term, 1857, Brannan sued to clear his own title and to set aside Mesick's deed as fraudulent. The court found for Brannan, basing its judgment on the Supreme Court ruling in the *Mesick* v. *Sunderland* litigation that the faulty description of the lots did not nullify the deed. Judge Monson declared that it was entitled to be recorded and had been recorded on July 20, 1850; payment of the $125,000 purchase price had also been made, or *what is a legal equivalent thereto* and had been duly acknowledged by young Sutter. The deed and registry were, consequently, considered in good order, and the court took great pains to prove that Mesick had had previous knowledge of the deed and its contents. His claim was declared a fraud, and a decree was entered in favor of Brannan.[148]

Nothing daunted, Mesick again appealed to the state's highest court. The trial commenced on July 24, 1857,[149] but a decision was delayed until the following May 25, partly because of the sudden death of Justice Murray. A notable trio of judges, Chief Justice Terry and Justices Peter H. Burnett[150] and Stephen J. Field, again reversed the decision of the lower court, though with qualifications not entirely favorable to Mesick. Changing its former stand, the court now ruled

---

[146] *Sacramento Union*, Oct. 6, 1856.

[147] *Ibid.*, Oct. 7, 1856.

[148] *Brannan* v. *Mesick*, in Labatt, *Reports*, I, 24–25; *Brannan* v. *Mesick*, in 6th Judicial Dist. Court (Sacramento), *Cases*, 2nd ser., nos. 2985, 3909 (1855).

[149] *Sacramento Union*, July 25, 1857.

[150] The same Burnett who had been agent for Sutter, Jr.

that Mesick bore the responsibility of enquiring into the validity of the previous deed. The court declared again, however, that the Brannan deed did not confer the title until certain conditions—chiefly, payment of the purchase price—had been fulfilled. The very existence of Mesick's deed was an indication that the Brannan group had never fulfilled those conditions. It was therefore necessary for Brannan to prove, in a new trial, that he and his associates had paid the purchase price fully and properly.[151] The following comment by the court suggests that this would not have been an easy task.

It is shown by the plaintiff's witness that the money was not, in fact, paid; that Sutter was induced to make a deduction of over forty thousand dollars, upon a representation that a portion of the property conveyed had been previously deeded away by Sutter, which representation, it appears, was not true. It also appears than an amount of money due Sutter on a former sale of lands, and secured by mortgage, was collected by Wetzlar under his power of attorney, and appropriated to the use of Brannan & Co., under the claim that the conveyance of June, 1850, had operated as an assignment of the debt.

The testimony of Wetzlar, one of the original parties to the deed, taken in connection with his manifest prevarication on many points, and the fact that his memory was totally at fault as to transactions concerning the same property in which he was personally engaged subsequent to the execution of the deed, while it was perfect as to the occurrences at the time of its execution, raise a strong presumption of fraud as to the settlement.[152]

It seemed doubtful that Brannan would be able to extricate himself from this new legal predicament, and his failure to do so is indicated by a brief notice in the *Sacramento Union* of July 2, 1858, stating that his petition to the Supreme Court had been denied and his bill dismissed. Thus ended a decade of land monopoly in Sacramento.

---

[151] *Brannan* v. *Mesick,* in *Calif. Reports,* X (1858), 95–109. The decision was delivered during the April term, 1858, but was included in the published reports for the July term, having been withheld pending the appeal for retrial. The opinion of the court, with the preliminary decision remanding the case for further proceedings, appeared also in the *Sacramento Union,* May 26, 1858.

[152] *Brannan* v. *Mesick,* in *Calif. Reports,* X (1858), 109.

A large part of the property had before this time passed into the hands of third parties, and the Supreme Court now declared that they possessed legal titles to the land if they had purchased in good faith. Many of them, however, had already paid Mesick to clear their titles. This is what the *Sacramento Union,* a consistent supporter of the Brannan case, had to say: *So far as innocent purchasers are involved, Mesick's title is not worth a straw. . . . This opinion of the Supreme Court will go far toward quieting titles in the city, and therein operate favorably upon her prosperity; but we suppose no decision, however righteous, will enable those who have been victimized by this Mesick claim to the amount of hundreds of dollars paid him to remove the cloud upon their titles, to recover back their money. Thousands of dollars have been extorted from our citizens. In some instances, one-half has been given to obtain the Mesick title to the other half of a lot. We trust such practices are now ended.*[153]

It is difficult to judge how much Mesick profited in land and in payments from third parties. Sutter, Jr., probably never received more than a few hundred dollars.[154]

Sutter's return to Acapulco was coincident with a critical moment in Mexico's turbulent history. Santa Anna, coming out of exile two years before, had, by means of wide promises and fat support of the army and the conservatives, once more seized the reins of dictatorship in Mexico. His regime, though full of pomp and circumstance, was quite empty of beneficial results. In the outlying states, strangers to the glitter of the capital, a murmur of resentment began to rise, chiefly in the liberal state of Guerrero, of which Acapulco was the chief port. There, in February, 1854, elderly General Juan Alvarez,[155] governor

---

[153] *Sacramento Union,* May 26, 1858.

[154] According to the Sutter-Mesick deed August received $51,500 for the Sacramento property and an additional $10,000 for the San Francisco property and any rights to the Alvarado and Micheltorena grants. (Sacramento County, *Deed Books,* vol. P, pp. 427–433). In *Brannan v. Mesick,* Brannan charged that Mesick actually paid August only $500. Mesick denied this, but Colonel Sanders, a witness in the case, believed it to be true. Judge Monson declared that Mesick paid but $500 for the conveyance, later adding another $900 and a bond for $25,000 to secure payment of a portion of the proceeds that he might realize from sales. (*Sacramento Union,* Apr. 8, 1857.)

[155] Alvarez, born in 1780, was chiefly responsible for the creation of the state

and political father of the state, raised the banner of revolt. Santa Anna moved quickly to quell it. His government, hoping to throttle the insurrection quickly at its source before it had time to spread to nearby states, decreed on February 13 that merchants, either Mexican or foreign, ordering goods from abroad for importation into any part of the territory held by the rebels were to be punished as conspirators. Less than three weeks later, on March 2, another decree ordered Acapulco closed to all trade.[156]

Nevertheless, the revolt was spreading and moving on toward success when young Sutter returned to Acapulco in 1855. His return would probably have passed unnoticed but for an unfortunate article which appeared in a San Francisco newspaper. When read in Acapulco it was immediately ascribed to young Sutter and resulted in an angry effort to send him out of the country. The move, bolstered and led, if not actually instigated, by Charles L. Denman, United States consul at the port, came in August, shortly after Sutter's arrival.

Rumor is flying fast, wrote "Frank,"[157] correspondent of the *Alta California,* on August 21, *that young Sutter, son of the old General, has been politically used and politely requested to leave this place by the next steamer, though he is lying dangerously ill at the present time.*

It appears that an extract of a letter written to the editor of the German paper of your city, and afterwards published in the Chronicle, *has given offence to some one here, and more particularly to the American consul; and at a meeting of five of the Generals, with the Governor and Consul, the latter urged and insisted strongly upon the banishment from the country of Sutter for the obnoxious article. After two days deliberation, the matter was postponed indefinitely;*

---

of Guerrero and became its first governor. He was uneducated but deeply imbued with republican views, and for nearly half a century was the undisputed ruler of the state, where, it was said, not a leaf could stir without his consent. His guerrilla forays from his home mountains during various revolutions earned him the title of "southern panther." An American correspondent wrote that "he is worshipped with true ardor and affection." (*Alta Calif.,* Sept. 13, 1855.) Hull's charge of mistreatment of the Rivas family seems to be the lone complaint against Alvarez.

[156] Bancroft, *Mexico,* V, 647–648.

[157] The elder Sutter identified him as Frank G. Senior in a letter of Sept. 18, 1855, to Samuel H. Harris. (U. S. State Dept., *Appointment Papers.*)

all acting favorably to Sutter with the exception of the Consul, to
whom Sutter had not a word to say, but in a frank and upright man-
ner denied to the others that he was the author of the letter. . . . In
the event of the Alvarez party being successful, this representative
[Denman] will be rewarded with a grant of land near this place of
much value. . . .

I saw young Sutter last evening, continued "Frank" on the twenty-
third, *and on yesterday and the day before, the American Consul was*
at the office of the Prefect, and insisted upon the papers necessary for
causing Sutter to be banished from the country.

Sutter says the Prefect told him this . . . and that he made a remark
in the presence of three others, that as soon as the war was concluded,
and he got his grant of land, he was going to resign his Consulship. I
trust, hope and pray that he may be removed before that time.[158]

A few days later the same correspondent wrote that Denman's efforts had failed and that he had called on Sutter disclaiming any part
in the plot against him.[159]

Unfortunately, it has not been possible to identify the article ascribed to Sutter, and the nature of the offending words must for the
present remain in question. It seems likely, however, that some scheme
of Denman and the Guerrero generals was shown in a poor light.[160]

---

[158] *Alta Calif.,* Sept. 3, 1855. "My son," wrote General Sutter, "is now in
possession of a certificate from a German Doctor (whose wife is from Acapulco)
resident in Sacramento City, that he is the author of said article." (Sutter to
Harris, Sept. 18, 1855, *op. cit.*)

[159] *Alta Calif.,* Sept. 13, 1855.

[160] In the *Calif. Chronicle* of June 22, 1855, appeared a short article translated from the *San Francisco Journal,* a German language paper. Entitled "The
Acapulco Expedition," it announced the imminent sailing of the English bark
Othello with a small group of men under a nephew of General Alvarez. The expedition was said to be interested only in peaceful development of the soil and
minerals of Guerrero, but the elder Sutter charged in his letter to Harris that it
was a scheme invented by Denman to lure Americans to Acapulco with reports
of rich gold mines. When they found no gold they were expected to enter the
services of Alvarez against Santa Anna. Some support for this charge is to be
found in a letter from Acapulco printed in the *Alta Calif.* of June 18, 1855, which
speaks of "the disappointed Acapulco gold hunters having joined the revolution-
ists and whipped out four or five times their number." Although the article spoke
of disorderly conditions in Guerrero, it was hardly offensive enough to have caused
such bitter resentment in Acapulco. Reference is made to another article in the

It is interesting to note that the consul made no mention of the incident in his official dispatches to Washington, and there is not a word of it in his records of the Acapulco consulate or in the records of the American embassy in Mexico City.[161]

Howard Joseph Sutter Hull, the grandson of August Sutter, writes of the animosity of General Alvarez toward the family of Sutter's wife. If true, it is rather curious that the governor did not avail himself of the opportunity presented by this incident to persecute the Rivas family through the son-in-law. It is possible, of course, that Alvarez was then too busily engaged for picayunish spites. Although Santa Anna chose not to prosecute a war in Guerrero's rugged mountains or along her malarial coast, believing that the rebellion would fall of its own weight, the rebel leader was actively pushing forward the revolt. In fact, he was eventually so successful that Santa Anna was forced to flee the country, and Alvarez himself, though seventy-five years old, was, on October 4, 1855, proclaimed ad interim president of Mexico.

It was anticipated that Denman would resign as consul when he received the land promised him by Alvarez, and, meanwhile, efforts were made to have Sutter, Jr., named to the post. As early as June 26, 1855, a group of prominent Californians urged President Franklin Pierce to make the appointment. This group included the elder Sutter's current agent, Colonel L. Sanders, Jr.; Richard Roman, former state treasurer; James A. McDougall, congressman from California; William M. Gwin, senator from California; J. W. Denver, a California congressman; Charles Fairfax, clerk of the state Supreme Court; John B. Weller, senator from California; and Joseph W. McCorkle, a former California congressman, then judge of the Ninth Judicial Court. The elder Sutter's letter of September 18 to Harris also urged his son's name.[162] These efforts, however, were premature, for not until ten years later did Washington recognize Sutter's position and capabilities and appoint him to the diplomatic service.

---

previous issue of the *Journal,* but unfortunately the Library of Congress copy is not now available for consultation because of war-time conditions, and no other copy has been located.

[161] P. M. Hamer, National Archives, to the writer, Aug. 27, 1941.

[162] U. S. State Dept., *Appointment Papers.*

August, having survived Denman's attack, settled down to recoup his lost California fortune. At about this time he joined the firm of Agustín Dempwolff & Co., which had established a small importing business under the name of El Bazar del Pacífico.[163] Though Sutter was without funds when he arrived in Acapulco, he was soon aided from two sources.

On her visit to California, María del Carmen had received as a gift from General Sutter a small amount of capital for her own use, but which *she employed in rehabilitating her husband's fortune.*[164] To this may be added what money he received from Mesick for the title to his California property. Whatever the amount, it is certain that August did have some actual cash to put into Dempwolff's business. Invigorated with the energy of the new partner, who was determined this time to make his business a success, and aided by the drastic tariff reduction declared in September, 1855,[165] the importing firm prospered as never before. On the death of Dempwolff in 1886, August became the principal owner.[166]

The Bazar itself was located near the beach, a block from the town's central plaza.[167] Close by, August built his house, a one-and-a-half story structure, which his father (who never saw it) declared to be *the best in the place.*[168] It was a large home built sturdily of stone in place of the more common adobe, and in the upper section the young merchant had his study, where he frequently retired to read, study, or write letters. There the children were never to disturb him. Surrounding the house were spacious grounds, shaded by numerous trees

---

[163] Mrs. Young to the writer, Oct. 25, 1942. On his burial vault the name appears as Augusto Carlos Luis Dempwolff, born in 1834.

[164] Hull to the writer, Feb. 21, 1941.

[165] *Alta Calif.,* Sept. 13, 1855.

[166] Mrs. Young to the writer, Oct. 25, 1942.

[167] Sutter's building no longer stands. The present building houses a laundry and numerous sidewalk shops. Reginaldo Sutter, son of a second marriage, states that his widowed mother held the Bazar until about 1910, when she sold it for 6,000 pesos. The owners of the exclusive Hotel La Marina, on the other side of the wide dirt street, now own the former Sutter property. (Smisor to the writer, July 25, 1941.)

[168] Sutter to Frederick W. Seward, Aug. 29, 1867, in U. S. State Dept., *Appointment Papers.*

and containing a large artificial pond, where Sutter each morning delighted to feed his ducks.[169]

It was here that Don Juan, as he came to be known in Acapulco, entertained many officers of the American warships which from time to time called at the port, including Admirals George F. Pearson and Henry K. Thatcher, Commodore Charles H. Poor, and Captain Gustavus H. Scott. In turn he was well received in their quarters afloat.[170] These friendships were later to pay Don Juan big dividends. Many prominent passengers of the Pacific Mail steamers, ashore for a few hours while their ships took on coal, were also invited to the Sutter residence.[171]

The Bazar was very much like a small-town general store in the United States. One American visitor, George E. Mills of San Francisco, arriving in Acapulco and seeking a way to Port Angels, was outfitted by Sutter with a small sailing whale boat, three Mexicans to row when the wind failed, and supplies of food and water for the three to six day trip. Mills stated that the crew was unable to find Port Angels, and that they had to put back into Acapulco after spending twelve days at sea. He charged that the provisions were full of worms and described Don Juan's Bazar as a *swindling grocery or dry good and variety Store where he does all kinds trading.*[172]

To balance this unfavorable estimate of Sutter's character and business methods we have a letter written by Gilbert M. Cole, American commercial agent at Acapulco, to his brother Cornelius, senator from California. Besides being well educated and very much of a gentleman, Sutter was honest and correct in business, Cole declared. *He is by far the most enterprising American citizen in Acapulco.*[173]

While John Sutter, Jr., was reshaping his life in Acapulco, his adopted Mexico was suffering the frightfulness of constant interne-

---

[169] Statement by Mrs. Young.

[170] Gilbert M. Cole to Cornelius Cole, Jan. 7, 1868, in U. S. State Dept., *Appointment Papers.*

[171] George E. Mills to President Grant, May 5, 1870, in U. S. State Dept., *Appointment Papers.*

[172] *Ibid.*

[173] G. M. Cole to C. Cole, Jan. 6, 1868, in U. S. State Dept., *Appointment Papers.*

cine strife. A parade of presidents followed old Juan Alvarez, who relinquished office on December 12, 1855, after a term of little more than two months. By 1861 the country was bankrupt, heavily in debt to European creditors, and torn by violence, class hatred, and corruption. The United States, involved in a bloody civil war, was in no position to uphold the Monroe Doctrine, and the stage was ideally set for foreign intervention. It was not long in coming. Spain, England, and France landed troops at Vera Cruz in the winter of 1861–62, though the Spanish and English soon withdrew. This left Emperor Louis Napoleon free to unfold his grandiose scheme for a great French-dominated empire in the New World. Pushing up from Vera Cruz, a strong French army in a succession of battles won most of Mexico, and French warships cruised along the coasts. Archduke Maximilian of Austria, handpicked by Napoleon and deceived by a controlled plebescite into believing that he was actually wanted by the Mexicans, arrived to accept a blood-born crown and unsteady throne as Emperor of Mexico.

Guerrero, lying behind its mountains, did not feel the first impact of the French invasion. Old Juan Alvarez, the "southern panther," and his Indian guerrillas were still supreme in their own rugged land, and the tranquil life of Acapulco was undisturbed. Then, on the morning of January 8, 1863, a French war steamer, the *Diamant,* appeared suddenly in Acapulco Harbor. An officer promptly called on General Diego Alvarez, son of Juan, and made three demands: that the *Diamant* be allowed to take on wood and water, that all harbor defenses be dismantled, and that the Mexicans apologize for having ordered a French warship out of the harbor several months before. Returning the next day for an answer, the officer was given the apology, but his first two demands were rejected, and the city began hasty preparations against the expected attack.

On the 10th a squadron under Admiral Bouét, consisting of the *Diamant,* the war steamer *Pallas,* and two corvettes, sailed up the bay and was immediately engaged by the forts. The squadron returned the fire and in two hours of heavy shelling succeeded in silencing all but one Mexican battery. During the bombardment a number of

French shells ripped into the town, firing some twelve houses and damaging perhaps fifty more.[174]

At this point, according to his grandson, Don Juan Sutter flashed into the picture. Enraged at what he thought to be deliberate, unnecessary damage to his adopted city, August leaped into a small boat, flung out the American flag, and, defying the danger of falling shot, headed out into the harbor. Boarding the French flagship, he sought out the admiral and, threatening him with the consequences of an international incident, demanded that he instantly cease firing on unarmed civilians. The admiral, declares Hull, immediately ordered the fire of his guns confined to the Mexican fort and fortín.[175]

During the two following days the French continued to pound at the one remaining Mexican battery, which, though too far away to do much damage, continued to spit shells at the attackers. French landing parties spiked a number of the inoperative guns below the fort and threw others into the sea, although a show of strong Mexican land forces kept them from penetrating the city. Finally, at 6 p. m. on January 12, after three days of bombardment Admiral Bouét despaired of silencing the lone Mexican battery or capturing the port, and retired. Each steamer took a corvette in tow, and the squadron dropped down the harbor and proceeded to sea.[176]

Sutter's amazing part in the defense of Acapulco, unfortunately, is difficult to verify with certainty. Bancroft, the western historian, merely reports that the French shelled the town for eight hours, doing considerable damage, and on the two following days fired on the fortifications, silencing three of them before retiring from the port.[177]

C. R. Payne, an eyewitness, declares that on January 9, when the *Diamant* retired after two of the French demands had been rejected, the American consul and the local agent of the Pacific Mail Steamship Co. went aboard the *Saranac,* a United States warship then in

---

[174] *Alta Calif.,* Jan. 27, 1863.

[175] Hull to the writer, Feb. 21, 1941.

[176] *Alta Calif.,* Jan. 27, 1863. Long descriptive letters from "Dios y Libertad," the paper's resident correspondent, and from C. R. Payne were printed in this issue.

[177] Bancroft, *Mexico,* VI, 60.

port. After a short stay aboard they proceeded down the bay for a conference with the French admiral, probably about the Pacific Mail steamers touching there. Upon his return that night, the agent visited the Mexican authorities to report on developments.[178]

Payne's statement gives some support to the Hull story when it is remembered that Don Juan, some time previous to 1866, had been in the employ of the steamship company. He was said to have been cashier and bookkeeper[179] and also to have acted as their Acapulco agent.[180] Reginaldo Sutter, when interviewed in Acapulco in the summer of 1941, recollected faintly that he had once heard such a story from an old sea captain but could not remember any details, and could not recall his father ever mentioning the incident.[181] Though this colorful story lacks conclusive proof, it must, in view of Sutter's later adventures and manifestations of courage, be given some mark of credence.

By 1865 Don Juan was apparently a figure of some importance in Acapulco business circles, for on July 22 of that year, Gilbert M. Cole, United States commercial agent, nominated him for vice-commercial agent at the port. This position required him to post a bond for $5,000. An anonymous letter from Acapulco to Washington later accused Cole of selling Sutter the office for $375, but Cole branded the charge a *whole cloth lie*.[182] During a short absence of Cole, from August 1 to September 9, Sutter was in charge of the agency. On August 12 the State Department in Washington approved Sutter's selection and a certificate of appointment was issued to him. He was re-appointed on January 5, 1866.[183]

---

178 *Alta Calif.*, Jan. 27, 1863.

179 Gilbert M. Cole, Despatch no. 33, May 7, 1866, in U. S. State Dept., *Consular Correspondence, Despatches.*

180 W. Rivas, W. Bevis, and others to State Dept., Feb. 12, 1868, in U. S. State Dept., *Appointment Papers.*

181 Smisor to the writer, July 25, 1941.

182 G. M. Cole to C. Cole, Jan. 7, 1868, in U. S. State Dept., *Appointment Papers.*

183 Details regarding his appointments are contained in a letter from E. Wilder Spaulding, State Dept., to the writer, Mar. 3, 1941; and in Hamer to the writer, Mar. 11, 1941; and Sutter, Jr., to William H. Seward, June 4, 1867, in U. S. State Dept., *Consular Correspondence, Despatches.*

Shortly after his second appointment Sutter became involved in an incident that added one more touch of color to his eventful life.

Porfirio Díaz, a fiery, vigorous leader of the Liberal forces, had been captured by the French at the fall of Oaxaca in February, 1865, and confined in Puebla. Fired by his country's desperate fight for freedom, Díaz immediately began working on some means of escape. Laboriously he dug a tunnel under his cell. Then he was moved. Another tunnel was slowly being scraped out when again he was transferred, this time to an upper room in the chapel of an old Caroline monastery. But to him there a dagger and four lariats were smuggled, and in the town a servant rented a house and bought two horses. In the darkness of the night of September 20, 1865, Díaz, lassoing an overhanging projection on the building, swung out and hauled himself up to the roof. Then silently crossing the roof, he knotted his four lariats together and slid safely to the ground. Stealthily working past the guards, he reached his horse, and in company with his servant galloped through the city gate into the night and headed westward. Next day a price of 11,000 pesos was put on his head, but, gathering supporters as he went, he succeeded in eluding pursuit and eventually reached the safety of Guerrero's mountains. There he was welcomed by old Juan Alvarez, who still held most of the state against the French and their Mexican allies.[184] Although the guerrilla troops were invincible in their mountain strongholds, Acapulco, the state's chief port, was now in the hands of Maximilian's men. The patriots in Guerrero were completely isolated from the other Liberal forces.

Then, on the night of April 20, 1866, Vice-Commercial Agent Sutter received a visitor—a mysterious woman visitor. He had hardly welcomed the stranger inside the house when there came a loud pounding on the door. Quickly the woman was shown into another room. Outside, Captain Lucido of the Mexican Imperial Garrison noisily demanded admittance to search for a young woman who had eluded him and was thought to have taken refuge with the American official. The Mexican officer, armed with a musket and later said to

[184] Beals, *Porfirio Díaz*, pp. 128–135; Creelman, *Díaz, Master of Mexico,* pp. 217–220.

have been partly intoxicated, was refused entrance. Sutter, knowing the desperate character of the man, who a minute before had broken a neighbor's door and shot at several persons, warned him not to force his way in. Nevertheless, the officer immediately began battering down the door with the butt of his musket, and Sutter, springing to a window, fired at him. The bullet tore harmlessly through the Mexican's hat, but it forced his hasty withdrawal, and he was thereupon arrested by his superiors and held for trial by court martial.

Some twenty-four hours later, when the officer's story had probably been heard, Sutter was requested to appear before the fiscal captain to make a statement. Suspecting nothing, so it is reported, he went to the magistrate's office, where he was arrested and incarcerated in San Diego Castle, which served as Acapulco's military prison.[185] But the officials had delayed too long. The prize, elusive Porfirio Díaz himself, still in woman's clothing, had escaped by boat in the night.[186]

Commercial Agent Cole immediately lodged a protest with General Apolonio Montenegro, commandant of the Mexican Imperial Garrison, and Sutter was finally released on bail, more than a fortnight after his arrest. Charges were still hanging over him when, on May 29, into Acapulco harbor steamed Commodore John Rodgers aboard the United States warship *Vanderbilt*, accompanied by the monitor *Monadnock*. Cole evidently lost no time in acquainting Commodore Rodgers with Sutter's plight and enlisting his aid, for during the brief stay of his frowning warships at Acapulco the commodore was able to effect Sutter's release from arrest *in a friendly and satisfactory manner*.[187]

The warships were scarcely gone when the impetuous Sutter was again in difficulties with the Mexican Imperial authorities. On July 7, 1866, he was left in charge of the American agency during the

---

[185] G. M. Cole, Despatch no. 33, in U. S. State Dept., *Consular Correspondence, Despatches;* Hamer to the writer, Aug. 27, 1941.

[186] The identification of this mysterious woman is made by Mrs. Anna Sutter Young. Díaz, escaping in the fall of 1865 to Guerrero, could still have been there in the spring of 1866.

[187] Hamer to the writer, Aug. 27, 1941.

absence of Gilbert Cole.[188] Sutter's open sympathy for the Liberal cause was well known, and despite his official status, his position became increasingly difficult. At last, aware that he was suspected of complicity in transmitting mail to the Liberals and that his position was now quite untenable, he hurriedly left town on October 14. The Imperialists threatened to shoot Sutter if they caught him, but he managed to escape. *I am told that Mr. Sutter, by making extra good time, and losing his hat and spectacles, succeeded in getting safely within the lines of the Liberalists,* Cole later reported to the State Department.[189]

Don Juan's escape left the Americans in Acapulco temporarily without an official representative. Taking matters into their own hands, they placed in charge of the agency one of their number, George M. Hedges, who served until Cole's return on November 16.[190] On October 17, but three days after Sutter's flight, Hedges was approached by the captain of the port, the chief of police, and a military officer, who requested him to open the mail bag addressed to the American consul at Acapulco in order that they might seize any correspondence directed to Sutter.[191] Hedges opened the bag, but the Mexicans found nothing. On the same day officials also seized the bag of the Wells Fargo Express Co. and the private pouch of the Pacific Mail Steamship Co. Most of the letters were returned to Hedges, but several retained by General Montenegro had been sent under cover of Sutter's name to General Diego Alvarez, President Juárez, and to other leaders of the Liberal government. Among those seized was one which gave an account of the shipment of arms to Alvarez on a schooner from San Francisco.[192]

By now, however, Maximilian's forces in Mexico were suffering reverses on all fronts. In February the French troops in Mexico began

---

[188] *Ibid.,* Mar. 11, 1941.

[189] G. M. Cole, Despatch no. 41, Nov. 16, 1866, in U. S. State Dept., *Consular Correspondence, Despatches.*

[190] Hamer to the writer, Mar. 11, 1941.

[191] This was the mail from the Pacific Mail steamer *Golden Age,* which left San Francisco Oct. 10, 1866, and reached Acapulco on the evening of the 17th. (*Alta Calif.,* Nov. 14, 1866.)

[192] Hamer to the writer, Aug. 27, 1941.

withdrawing to Vera Cruz preparatory to leaving the country, and on February 18, 1867, the Mexican Imperialists evacuated Acapulco. Some time after the evacuation, Don Juan returned to the port.[193]

Because of ill health, Cole gave up his Acapulco office on May 17, 1867. He left Sutter once more in charge, paying him out of his own pocket.[194] On July 22, 1868, Sutter was appointed United States commercial agent. His friends, however, wished to have him made a full consul and bent their influence to that end. Their letters of recommendation addressed to President Johnson and the two Sewards in the State Department soon began to arrive in Washington. The first, dated July 25, 1866, was signed by six senators, including James A. McDougall of California. A year later Sutter was recommended by three Californians: Frank Soulé, collector of the first district, L. C. Gunn, assessor of the same, and John Bidwell, one of the really honest friends of his father. At intervals during the following two years other letters were written by Cornelius Cole, newly elected senator from California, old General Sutter, General Diego Alvarez, successor to his father as the all-powerful governor of Guerrero, and various groups of American and Mexican residents and merchants of Acapulco.[195]

Sutter had served as commercial agent for nearly two years when the State Department reëstablished a full consulate, making him consul of the Acapulco port and district. His commission, signed by President Grant and Secretary of State Hamilton Fish, was dated July 13, 1870. On November 4, the American minister in Mexico City presented Sutter's name to the Mexican Secretary for Foreign Affairs, who replied the next day that President Benito Juárez had authorized the issuance of the requested exequatur, officially approving the appointment.[196]

---

193 *Ibid.*

194 G. M. Cole to C. Cole, Jan. 6, 1868, in U. S. State Dept., *Appointment Papers.*

195 U. S. State Dept., *Appointment Papers.*

196 Mexico. Ministerio de Relaciones Exteriores. Paquete: Cónsules extranjeros, Número 31, 1870. Estados Unidos, Sutter, John A., Cónsul, Acapulco, 44–20–122; Hamer to the writer, Mar. 11, 1941; Spaulding to the writer, Mar. 3, 1941.

This position Sutter was to hold until his own resignation seventeen years later. Regulations of the State Department did not permit him now, as consul, to engage in private business,[197] and therefore Dempwolff managed the firm until his death on February 10, 1886.[198] Sutter was then obliged to take in new partners to run El Bazar del Pacífico for him. These were Pedro Kastan, his son Enrique and one Rivera.[199]

His chief duty as consul, of course, was the promotion of trade with the United States. He evidently did all that was required of him toward this end. He wrote reports on such topics as citrus culture, cotton production, commercial credit, leather tanning and the boot and shoe industry in Guerrero. But his efforts frequently were without result. R. H. Loughery, who succeeded him as consul, once wrote: *My predecessor, in his reports, called attention to the fact that the trade here could be largely increased if those* [American exporters] *seeking it would put up their goods in a different manner and with other suggestions that were valuable, all of which have been unheeded.*[200]

Acapulco, however, had long ago lost the commercial glory it had known as the terminus of the famed Manila galleon trade. By the time Sutter came to reside there it was of little economic consequence; he once reported to the State Department that its population and that of the vicinity *rely for a livelihood exclusively on the traffic caused by the steamers of the Pacific Mail Steamship Company.*[201] The rugged mountains eastward effectively cut the town off from all but desultory traffic by steep trails with the interior. So difficult and precipitous was the three-hundred-mile trail to Mexico City, ten days by horseback, that it was referred to as *un buen camino de pájaros,* a good road for birds.[202] Situated on a small rise overlooking Santa

---

[197] *Official Register of the U. S., 1883,* I, 21, 26.

[198] Smisor to the writer, July 25, 1941.

[199] Statement by Mrs. Young; Mrs. Young to the writer, Oct. 25, 1942.

[200] *Commercial Relations of the U. S., 1886 and 1887,* p. 586.

[201] *Ibid., 1875,* p. 1137.

[202] Wells, "Economic Study of Mexico," in *Popular Science Monthly,* XXIX (1886), 157.

Lucía Bay, Acapulco, with its narrow, crooked little dirt streets and
its brown adobe buildings, slept out the warm, windless years beside
its wasting harbor. At the end of June the eagerly awaited rains came.
By the end of October some fifty inches had usually fallen, renewing
the sunbaked earth and reviving the parched plant life. During the
most pleasant season, December and January, the temperature rarely
rose above 90° Fahrenheit, but in the latter part of the dry season the
heat over the land was intense.

Many years before he gained fame as an archaeologist, Heinrich
Schliemann called at Acapulco on March 22, 1851, en route to California. He reported that a French engineer had drained the swamp
and made a large cut in the hill to the west, allowing the wind to
blow through, thus considerably improving the health of the town.[203]
The cut did not solve the problem completely, but it was years before
the Acapulcans again got around to doing something about the hot,
close air.

About the middle of the 1880's, Don Juan Sutter (who had once
complained about a Sacramento summer) and other prominent residents of the town encouraged Colonel Lopetegui, *jefe de la plaza*, to
hack out of the high western peninsula forming Acapulco's harbor
a long cut to the sea breezes on the other side. Lopetegui, with a
company of soldiers, slowly and laboriously made a slit about fifty feet
wide, as many deep, and a thousand feet long, which now allows a
strong cool afternoon breeze to blow over part of the town. But this
canal de aereación was never completed. Some time after 1890 Lopetegui was transferred while still a thirty-meter depth remained to be
cut, and no successor has since carried on the work.[204]

It was in this drowsy land that Don Juan Sutter was to pass the
remainder of his life, apparently in some ease and contentment, but
not without involvement in local events that gravely concerned the
lives of the people. Don Juan, through his dual position of American
consul and old Mexican resident, was destined to play some role in

---

[203] *Schliemann's First Visit to America, 1850–1851*, p. 48.

[204] Smisor to the writer, July 25, 1941; he also reports that it is now slowly
filling up again with dirt and rubble.

any activity that momentarily shook the sleep out of Acapulco's eyes. The incidents are worth noting.

In 1876 Mexican politics once more boiled over when Porfirio Díaz led an insurrection against President Lerdo de Tejada. On November 16, General Alatorre's loyal forces were crushed. Lerdo fled to Acapulco and thence to the United States, leaving the way open for Díaz' triumphal advance into Mexico City. The conqueror then ordered a national election, at which he was very naturally elected to the office he had already assumed, and on May 2, 1877, he was officially proclaimed president.

Lerdo resistance, disconnected, scattered, and ineffectual, continued in some of the outlying sections of Mexico. In the south General Diego Alvarez, true son of the old "southern panther," gathered together his Indian forces and on May 27, 1877, attacked General Jiménez, of the Díaz faction, in Acapulco. Jiménez resisted fiercely, but within half an hour he was bottled up in Fort San Diego, where he continued to fire at Alvarez and his thousand Indians who firmly held the town.

Then, from the harbor, the Porfirista gunboat *México,* in an effort to dislodge the insurrectionists, began throwing shells into the town, destroying houses and killing a number of defenseless civilians. The American merchants in the port hastily carried their papers and other valuables to the consulate for safekeeping. Sutter himself immediately went into action. In a move reminiscent of his bold course during the French bombardment of 1863, he quickly interposed, *and made such representations to the Mexican commander as to cause a cessation of the shelling that day.*

Firing, however, was renewed the next day, May 28, and *the Consul and merchants again interceded to save the town and prevent the slaughter of innocent people, and after three days' negotiations succeeded in arranging for cessation of hostilities until the Government should agree upon terms of settlement.* Though Alvarez had already begun ousting local officials and replacing them with staunch Lerdistas, he surrendered the town in a few days to the gunboat's commander. Díaz was not long in coming to terms. About the middle of June, Don Rafael Cuéllar arrived from Mexico City at the head of a strong force of soldiers, bearing in his pocket a commission as governor of Guerrero, superseding the recalcitrant Alvarez.[205]

The Porfiristas had had their eyes on the American consul in Acapulco despite his personal friendship with Díaz himself. Evidently incensed at what they thought was Sutter's interference in the affair, they cast him into jail, thus repeating the indignity of 1866. There he languished until once more, like the galloping rescue in the old silent cinema, the timely arrival of an American warship brought him freedom.

The story is told in several San Francisco papers, which received it from the United States sloop-of-war *Pensacola,* upon her arrival in that city on June 30:

When the Pensacola *arrived at Acapulco, Consul Sutter was lying in jail, and a demand was made for his release, the payment of damages, and the paying of a salute to the Stars and Stripes. The Consul was at once released, but he declined insisting upon damages as there would be nothing to pay them with in any event. The day after the Díaz party, led by the younger General Jiménez, appeared in the plaza opposite the Consul's residence, accompanied by a battery of field pieces, and when the American flag was being hoisted on its staff saluted it with the Consular salute of seven guns, all of which healed the wounded honor of the Consul and the flag.*[206]

In a more prosperous country, perhaps, or in a country more conscious of its local heroes, a statue in the public square would today honor Don Juan Sutter as the savior of the town. For he had twice saved Acapulco from destruction by the flaming guns of hostile vessels—and twice he himself had been rescued from the dungeon by the frowning guns of friendly ones.

Sutter's activity in this affair evidently resulted in some disapproval, for an undercover attempt to have him removed from office may be inferred from a petition of August 25, 1877, strongly urging

---

[205] *Alta Calif.,* June 16, 27, 28, 1877; Creelman, in *Díaz, Master of Mexico,* p. 359, declares that Alvarez' opposition was peacefully overcome by the president's persuasive reasoning.

[206] *San Francisco Chronicle,* July 1, 1877; *Daily Evening Post,* July 2, 1877.

his retention. The signers, among the strongest business firms in San Francisco, were Williams Blanchard Co., agents of the Pacific Mail Steamship Co., William T. Coleman & Co., Parrott & Co., and J. C. Merrill & Co.[207] The ouster attempt came to naught and does not seem to have been the result of any widespread feeling against the consul.

Another incident, in which Don Juan took a prominent part, furnishes further evidence of the great change in his strength of will since the Sacramento period. Unlike the inexperienced boy, who had been the dupe of conspiring men, August in his Acapulco days manifested both initiative and courage. Gilbert Cole said once that Sutter was *known to be a fearless & brave man in defence of a right.*[208] His interest in the public welfare, indicated by his gift of public squares to the city of Sacramento, was shown in Acapulco to be really a deep concern for the common people. The story comes from his grandson, Howard Joseph Sutter Hull.

According to Hull, some Spanish commercial houses had a monopoly on corn. Sutter sent his sailing vessels to Guaymas for a supply and threatened to give it to the starving people if the merchants did not reduce their price to cost. This they did, rather than risk a total loss by holding it in storage where it might spoil. Shortly thereafter, Sutter was arrested by the colonel in command of the fort and thrown into jail. When the colonel notified Díaz of this action the president telegraphed him to release the prisoner immediately. Sutter, however, would not be freed without an apology and a salute to the American flag, and the colonel once more had to ask Díaz for instructions. The answer came back: *Apologize and salute.*[209]

The date of this incident is uncertain. Acapulco, it must be understood, was closely dependent upon its own corn harvests, and crop failures resulted in two severe famines during Sutter's period of office. In his consular report of September 30, 1875, to Washington, he wrote that the near total failure of the cotton crop as well as the total

---

[207] U. S. State Dept., *Appointment Papers.*
[208] G. M. Cole to C. Cole, Jan. 7, 1868, in U. S. State Dept., *Appointment Papers.*
[209] Hull to the writer, Feb. 21, 1941.

failure of the corn crop, upon which the entire population relied, had been the cause of dire famine and suffering among the poorer classes of the district. It was necessary to import corn from Mazatlán and San Francisco.[210]

It was during this time of famine and suffering, too, that gangs of thieves and assassins, encouraged by the dire straits of the people and under cover of political dissensions, frequently threatened violence. For nearly two months, during August and September of 1876, there was serious danger of a mob uprising in Acapulco to plunder and murder the town's wealthier inhabitants, including, of course, the Sutters and a number of foreign residents. When the highest civil authority of the district declared publicly its inability to cope with the situation, the merchants, both native and foreign, promptly banded together and took protective measures of their own. Business houses were barricaded, and armed garrisons were employed for night duty. Only this determined and unified action, declared Consul Sutter, prevented a serious outbreak.[211]

Another severe corn shortage occurred ten years later, and on June 1, 1886, Sutter wrote that *though the merchants of Acapulco try to lessen the famine by importing considerable quantities of corn, rice, flour, &c., from San Francisco, many families have no means for the purchase of the so much needed corn, and live nearly naked, on fruit of all kinds and edible roots growing wild in the woods.*[212]

Sutter's part in the corn famine seems to be well known, writes George T. Smisor. *Reginaldo says that Don Juan did force the price down, and was thrown into jail, fined 30,000 pesos (which of course he did not pay) and through protest was able to force the Mexican gunboat in the harbor at that time to give him a 21-gun salute when he was let out of jail.*[213] Unfortunately neither Hull nor Reginaldo

---

[210] *Commercial Relations of the U. S., 1875,* p. 1136.

[211] *Ibid., 1876, pp.* 752–753. Ernestina Sutter Morlett, daughter of Sutter's son Reginaldo, remembers playing as a child in a large subterranean tunnel which her grandfather had built under the Bazar for the storage of goods. (Smisor to the writer, July 25, 1941.) The construction of such a tunnel may have been one of Sutter's own precautions against the threat of fire or pillage.

[212] *Commercial Relations of the U. S., 1884 and 1885,* p. 675.

[213] Smisor to the writer, July 25, 1941.

Sutter indicate with which of the famines this incident is connected.

An interesting point in Hull's account of Sutter's participation in the corn famine is his statement that his grandfather sent his own sailing vessels to Guaymas for corn. If this were true, Sutter must have owned the major part of Acapulco's merchant fleet, for he himself wrote in 1873: *The shipping interests of the port of Acapulco are insignificant, consisting of only three schooners and two sloops.*[214] In 1887 his consular successor reported that Acapulco had only two vessels belonging to the port, one a schooner of forty tons and the other a sloop of fifteen.[215] Despite Hull's statement, it hardly seems likely that Sutter owned any part of the meager Acapulco fleet, unless, possibly, in his wife's name;[216] for as consul at Acapulco (he received $2000 a year, the second highest American consular salary in Mexico) he was not permitted to engage in private business.

Sometime before 1862 Sutter and his first wife were separated. The exact circumstances are not known, but for some reason they were never divorced.[217] María del Carmen is said to have moved to San Francisco, and perhaps at that time she took the other two children, Anna Eliza and María del Carmen, to Hock Farm to join little John III in the care of the elder Sutters. At any rate, the three children were taken east by the general and his wife a few years later and were put in school there.[218] Their mother lived during her later years with John III in Brooklyn and died there in 1898.[219]

---

[214] *Commercial Relations of the U. S., 1873,* p. 822.

[215] *Ibid., 1886 and 1887,* p. 584.

[216] "One thing seems to be common knowledge and it is the fact that neither Doña Nicolasa nor Don Juan ever owned any ships." (Concha J. Hudson to the writer, Apr. 21, 1942.)

[217] Zollinger, *Sutter,* pp. 321, 329; Smisor to the writer, July 25, 1941. María del Carmen seems to have initiated the separation. George Mills, whose word can hardly be credited, declared that she left because Sutter "gave her such a awful beating that she was at the point of death." (Mills to President Grant, May 5, 1870, in U. S. State Dept., *Appointment Papers.*) Mrs. Young stated, simply, that María deserted him and, her whereabouts being unknown to Sutter, he was unable to obtain a divorce. No mention of the marriage was made in 1942 in connection with a suit instituted by the Sutter heirs claiming compensation for the loss of Los Organos. ("Claim for Expropriation of Property in Mexico," Aug. 19, 1942, in Sutter, Jr., Papers.)

[218] Additional information about the children is given in Appendix I.

[219] According to a letter from James W. Henderson, of the Green-Wood Cem-

About the year 1870[220] Sutter formed a union with Nicolasa Solís, with whom he lived for the rest of his life. Such left-handed marriages were quite common in Mexico then, largely because most young people could not pay the fee for a legal ceremony.[221] Sutter's reason, however, probably was that he had not been divorced from María del Carmen, to whom he seems to have been married both in the church and by civil ceremony.[222] It was only in 1894, three years before his death, that he took steps to legalize his marriage with Doña Nicolasa.[223]

Their son Reginaldo declared in 1941 that his parents were married in the Catholic Church in 1870, and that the civil ceremony of 1894 was performed to comply with new laws.[224] In 1873 a Mexican reform law decreed that marriage was a civil contract and gave exclusive jurisdiction over it to the civil authorities.[225] Nevertheless, Reginaldo's statement is not entirely convincing. Miss Concha J. Hudson, of the American consular staff at Acapulco, has interviewed many people who knew the Sutter family well and she has this to say: *It seems to be a well known fact around the town that Sutter married Nicolasa Solís without having divorced his first wife. There is even a peculiar story about the procedure taken in getting the second marriage recorded in the civil books.* Unfortunately, she does not relate this story.[226]

Nicolasa was the niece of General Solís and was said to have been a school teacher, although she was unable to sign her own name to

---

etery, she died on Mar. 11, 1898, at the age of sixty-two. If this figure is correct she was a girl of fourteen when she married Sutter.

[220] Cristina, eldest of the known children, was born in 1874. In 1897 Sutter wrote in his will that for twenty-five years Nicolasa had been forming a little patrimony for their children, apparently pushing the date back at least to 1872. Reginaldo said they were married in 1870.

[221] See John W. Dwinelle, "Diary," in Soc. Calif. Pioneers, *Quarterly,* VIII (1931), 160.

[222] Hudson to the writer, Apr. 21, 1942; Hull to the writer, Feb. 21, 1941.

[223] On Apr. 13, 1894. A transcript of the record in the *Juzgado del Estado Civil (Registro Civil, Libro 3)* is in the possession of the writer.

[224] Reginaldo Sutter to Mabel R. Gillis, California State Librarian, Feb. 17, 1934.

[225] Foster, *Diplomatic Memoirs,* I, 49.

[226] Hudson to the writer, Apr. 21, 1942.

her marriage certificate. Sutter met her at a Fourth of July banquet for local Americans. Nicolasa, who had been hired, as she supposed, in the capacity of a hostess, broke into tears when she was ordered to wait on table, whereupon the gallant guests, including Sutter, arose in protest and refused to eat until the matter had been adjusted to the girl's satisfaction.[227] Nicolasa was born in 1850, the year Sutter came to Acapulco, and was about twenty when they began living together. She bore nine children to Sutter.[228]

It was in Doña Nicolasa's name that the Sutters acquired their considerable holdings of land. In 1855 they acquired on November 24 a tract of a little more than two square miles, on the banks of the Río de la Sabana. The next year adjoining areas were added, more than doubling the size of the property and taking in both sides of the river. Another small parcel was added in 1888.[229] All of this formed Sutter's well known Los Organos Rancho, some twelve miles east of Acapulco, a large, fertile tract of land which could be irrigated from the river and from several wells and spring-fed streams.[230]

Accounts differ on how Sutter acquired the rancho. Miss Concha J. Hudson and her mother, a lifelong resident of the town, believe that it was a gift of appreciation from one of the Alvarez generals, probably Diego, for favors received. Reginaldo Sutter firmly contended, however, that his mother purchased the property, buying the first part for 5,000 pesos and later adding to it, the total cost being 20,000 pesos.[231] His sister, Mrs. Anna Sutter Young, states that the property was purchased in later years, after the failure of her father's store. Her mother then, she declares, sold all her jewels and valuables, realizing enough to purchase 5,000 hectares, or about 12,000 acres.

On Los Organos, Sutter grew limes, pineapples, and sugar cane,

---

[227] Statement by Mrs. Young.

[228] The number given in Sutter's will. See Appendix I for additional information about the children.

[229] Map of rancho, 1894, in Sutter, Jr., Papers. Additions to the property were made on Apr. 6, June 9, and Sept. 14, 1886, and on June 1, 1888.

[230] "Los Organos Rancho is a very large and beautiful piece of property. It is now traversed by the highway to Mexico City, and one passes through the little village of Los Organos about 15 miles from Acapulco." (Smisor to the writer, July 25, 1941.)

[231] *Ibid.*

and Hull, who as a boy lived in the Sutter home in Acapulco, suggests that perhaps he also raised a few hundred head of cattle. The fruit products were shipped to San Francisco in the holds of fast Pacific Mail steamers, which regularly called at Acapulco for coal, stores, and the irregular Mexican subsidy. Doña Nicolasa, relieving her busy husband of many of the ranch burdens, was unusually active for a woman in Mexico and pushed the development of the plantation energetically. Particularly noteworthy among her achievements was the planting and cultivating of extensive lime orchards, said to be the first in Acapulco, though the wild tree was native to the region.[232] Limes imported from Acapulco orchards still add their touch to the alcoholic bracers of present-day Californians.

By 1887 Don Juan had been a resident of Acapulco for nearly thirty-seven years. During that time he had come to love the little port lying in its sheltered bay by the warm Pacific, surrounded by a wild, rugged hinterland that almost isolated it from the interior. Writing of the depression of 1875 to the State Department, which was accustomed to bald economic accounts banked with tables of statistics, Sutter, for the first time in his printed reports, showed something of his real feelings for the city of his adoption. The inclusion of just one adjective, the word "beautiful," brings the only bit of color and feeling into his usually dry, objective reports. *The present state of affairs cannot change for the better,* he wrote, *until the agricultural and mining interests of this really beautiful and rich country shall commence to be developed.*[233] In these lines one may read the affection of a man for the town which had been his home for more than half his life.

---

[232] Reporting on *Orange and Lemon Culture in Guerrero,* Sutter wrote of the lime: "This tree is indigenous, whilst the other varieties of the citrus family are said to have been imported." (U. S. State Dept., *Consular Reports,* no. 41½, June, 1884, p. 777.) Hull, writing of Sutter's first wife, declares: "She was a very able, energetic woman who started the Lime Orchards in Acapulco which was a source of income to many people in the surrounding country." (Hull to the writer, Feb. 21, 1941.) This, of course, is erroneous, since María del Carmen was no longer living with Sutter when he acquired agricultural lands. Both the Hudsons are certain that it was Doña Nicolasa who planted the lime trees. So also was Reginaldo Sutter, who declared that at one time there were 20,000 lime trees on the Sutter property, yielding some 20,000 boxes of fruit a month during the season. (Smisor to the writer, July 25, 1941.)

[233] *Commercial Relations of the U. S., 1875,* p. 1137.

Sutter had been a foreign official for nearly twenty-one years when, on May 24, 1887, he at last retired and was succeeded by R. W. Loughery of Texas.[234] Now in his sixty-first year, Sutter retired to his plantation on the Sabana River to spend his declining years. The recollections of his grandson Hull picture him as a very near-sighted old gentleman with white hair. Despite a rather irascible spirit, he was well liked by the Mexican people, and today elderly citizens of Acapulco still remember him respectfully as Don Juan. A white beard and moustache gave him a distinguished appearance, and, unlike his father, he did not gain much weight during his last years.[235]

It will be remembered that after the death of Dempwolff, in 1886, Sutter had been obliged to take new partners into the Bazar. The business had prospered while he was in charge, but when he accepted the consulship endless troubles began. Rivera was much too liberal with credit and allowed poor accounts to stack up, and, according to Mrs. Young, Kastan proved dishonest. Most of the papers pertaining to Sutter's business have been lost, many when a mob burned the ranch house at Los Organos, and those still in the possession of Mrs. Young shed little light on the situation.

Enough remain, however, to show that there was considerable trouble with Kastan. In July, 1889, he brought Sutter into court to account for his disbursement of the company's funds. Evidently Kastan had some success, for Sutter wrote to the new consul on January 11, 1890: *On the 6th day of this present month, at 8 o'clock in the morning, the aforesaid First Judge of the Minor Court of this city, accompanied by the Prefect of this District, his police and the said Kastan, came to the business store styled "Bazar del Pacifico," where I had placed a capital of $60,000, and there, perforce of brute violence, threats &c broke in the doors of the house, and took the said money, thus constituting a penal offence.*[236] It seems that the store had been closed, so that neither Kastan nor Sutter could enter until the case had been settled. Sutter claimed that justice had been denied

[234] Hamer to the writer, Mar. 11, 1941; *Official Register of the U. S., 1887,* I, 29.

[235] Hull to the writer, Feb. 21, 1941; statement by Smisor.

[236] Sutter, Jr., Papers.

him, and he asked the consul to submit his papers to Washington, hoping that the Mexican government could be made to indemnify him for the lost $60,000.

Writing to the American minister in Mexico City on January 13, 1890, he declared further: *The parties interested in this suit not only took possession of the store, with all its contents, breaking into the house by violence, and engaging an armed police to guard it, but they have since sold all the goods. . . . My interest in these goods amounts to about $30,000. Unless I obtain relief, it involves me almost a financial ruin.*[237]

It is not known how the matter was finally adjusted, but on October 3, 1894, in a settlement of the affairs of A. Dempwolff Successors, by which name the firm had become known, Kastan ceded to Sutter an additional half square mile of land adjoining the Sabana rancho. This new parcel was the most level of the entire rancho, was situated in a fertile triangle along the river, and included the little town of Los Organos.[238]

Ailing, and fretting over his business, Sutter, according to his daughter Anna, at one time became so discouraged that he even talked of suicide as a way out of his physical and mental misery. The thought of Doña Nicolasa and the unprotected young children deterred him. It may have been at this time that Nicolasa sold her jewels as a means of reëstablishing her husband and insuring the future of the children.

Don Juan never regained the prosperity he had enjoyed in former years. He had not been very well for some time and he was now too ill to prosecute his business properly. On April 13, 1894, at long last, he married the faithful Doña Nicolasa, and less than two weeks later gave her his power of attorney to carry on his business for him.[239] Then, just ten years after resigning his consulship and retiring to his rancho, Sutter's health completely failed, and he moved into Acapulco to his house at Calle Bravo 3. Feeling himself gradually growing weaker, he called to his bedside a notary public, and at 11:30 on

---

[237] *Ibid.*

[238] Map of rancho, 1894, in Sutter, Jr., Papers.

[239] Sutter, Jr., Papers.

the morning of September 6, 1897, began dictating his will. It covered six points:

1. He professed the Calvinist faith and ordered that his funeral be conducted according to the rites of that religion.

2. He stated that he was leaving the necessary funds for taxes and other requirements of law.

3. He declared that he was married civilly to Mrs. Nicolasa Solís, and acknowledged six living children: Cristina, Reginaldo, Rosa Sofía, Alfredo, Juan, and Anita, the first two of age, and the rest minors. Three others had died.

4. He declared that he had lost the property which he possessed at the time of his marriage to Mrs. Solís because his health had not allowed him to attend to his business properly.

5. He declared that his wife, Mrs. Nicolasa Solís, had formed a small patrimony for their children, and that all existing properties were to be *of their pure and genuine ownership without any exception.*

6. His wife was named his executrix.[240]

The document was signed by two of his employees and a merchant friend.

Fifteen days later, on September 21, 1897, just short of his seventy-first birthday, John August Sutter, Jr., died. Within twenty-four hours, to conform to the time limit of Mexican law, he was placed in the pretentious family vault in the Panteón Municipal.[241] Today, high in his crypt, overlooking the wild, unkept shrubbery of the Panteón, Don Juan lies behind a painted, fast-peeling inscription:

JUAN A. SUTTER
De origen Suizo y consul americano
durante 24 años en este puerto.
Falleció a la edad de 72 años.

---

[240] "Second Copy of the Testament Made by John A. Sutter, [Jr.,] prepared for Mrs. Anna Sutter de Young, Acapulco, Oct. 22nd, 1924," in Sutter, Jr., Papers.

[241] Hull to the writer, Feb. 21, 1941; Smisor to the writer, July 25, 1941; Hamer to the writer, Mar. 11, 1941; Reginaldo Sutter to Mabel R. Gillis, California State Librarian, Feb. 17, Mar. 1, 1934.

Su esposa e hijos le dedican este recuerdo.

Acapulco Sep. 21 de 1897[242]

After her husband's death, Doña Nicolasa hired a manager to look after her business affairs. The papers still extant indicate that her financial road was at times a rocky one, for she was obliged to borrow money in 1910. In January, 1914, Maximino San Millán was pressing her for payment of a debt of 7,000 pesos, for which she had given as security the Palo Blanco part of the Los Organos property, and one half of the Bravo Street house.[243] Nearly two years later she offered to withdraw all her claims against the city of Sacramento if the city would lift a mortgage of $11,000 from her property in Mexico.[244] Nothing was done about this offer, but she was evidently able to clear at least the major portion of the Los Organos Rancho, for it was divided among the children after her death in 1922.

By virtue of her marriage to Sutter in 1894, Nicolasa became an American citizen and remained one for the rest of her life. In 1914, when feeling in Mexico ran high against the United States and many American citizens were beaten and even killed by angry peons, a mob descended one night upon Los Organos. Señora Sutter met them alone on the veranda and vainly sought to quiet them. In the middle of her tongue-lashing, she warned: *This is American property.* It was a courageous but unfortunate thing to say. The fury of the mob immediately rose to a new pitch, and they soon broke up into gangs bent upon destruction of the plantation. Before her eyes the lime trees were felled, the sugar mill was put to the torch, excited cattle were caught and slaughtered, and the ranch house, in which she and Don Juan had spent their declining years, was partially destroyed. Threatened by violent madmen who swarmed into the house, Doña Nicolasa, her daughter Anna, and several grandchildren seized what few things they could carry in their arms and fled to Acapulco, where they took the first steamer to San Francisco. The rest of their

---

[242] Smisor to the writer, July 25, 1941.

[243] Sutter, Jr., Papers.

[244] *Sacramento Bee,* Oct. 13, 1916. This was probably the mortgage to San Millán.

personal property was destroyed, including many of Don Juan's papers and books.[245]

About June, 1915, they moved to Sacramento at the solicitation of one Valentine Arsega, who encouraged Nicolasa in the belief that she had inherited property rights there from her husband. She felt that by erecting schools on the blocks which Sutter, Jr., had given for public use, the city had broken the conditions of the gift, and that the property should revert to his heirs. She also believed that she had certain claims to Sutter's Fort and the ground on which it stood. In December, 1915, Nicolasa, in a power of attorney to Paul H. Steude, gave him the right to sue the city.[246] Then, late the following year, she offered to give the city a clear title in return for lifting the mortgage on her property in Mexico. Nothing came of this plan, and Señora Sutter, weary and dispirited, returned to San Francisco. Recalling that period in Sacramento, her daughter Anna wrote: *My mother and I came to Sacramento as refugees from the Mexican revolution, to the city that had been practically founded by my father, and so greatly benefitted by him in his donations of land for public parks. Instead of affording us some sort of recognition, the city literally closed its doors on us.*[247]

When Anna married in 1920, Señora Sutter was taken into their home, along with the four motherless children of another daughter. Then in February, 1922, dying of dropsy and heart trouble, the seventy-two-year-old widow of Sacramento's founder addressed a pathetic letter to the Native Daughters of the Golden West. She recounted her husband's generosity to the city of Sacramento, and as his widow, pleaded for assistance from patriotic Californians. She was penniless and could not afford a doctor.[248] The Sacramento parlors of both the Native Daughters and the Native Sons promised immediate help, but it was the Sacramento Rotary Club which on Feb-

---

[245] Statement by Mrs. Young.

[246] *Sacramento Bee,* Aug. 18, Dec. 10, 20, 1915. The school lots were those bounded by Fifteenth, Sixteenth, I and J Streets and Ninth, Tenth, P and Q Streets.

[247] Mrs. Young to the writer, Oct. 25, 1942.

[248] *Sacramento Bee,* Feb. 15, 1922.

ruary 16 subscribed nearly $300 for her immediate relief. The dying woman was placed in a hospital and a Spanish-speaking nurse was hired for her. Two days later, on February 18, Nicolasa Solís Sutter died. The newspapers record that the grand officers of the Native Sons of the Golden West acted as pallbearers at her funeral.[249]

Following Señora Sutter's death, the Los Organos Rancho was divided among the children.[250] At least two attempts were made by the heirs to rehabilitate the property, but in each case their work was destroyed and they were forced off the ranch.[251] After 1926 none of the Sutters appear to have resided at Los Organos[252] and they were thus in the position of absentee landlords. The *ayuntamiento* of Acapulco, complying with the request of a group of Mexican agrarians or *campesinos,* declared on October 19, 1929, that the property was vacant, unused, and subject to seizure. A few days later a large number of Mexicans, emulating in a small way the Oklahoma boomers of 1889, swarmed onto the rancho and staked out their small farms. The Sutters lodged immediate complaints with the *ayuntamiento,* various state officials, and even the governor of Guerrero, but without avail. In so far as the local officials are concerned the case is now closed, for they report that the protests have been destroyed and that no evidence exists in their files. The rancho is considered one of the *ejido* projects, encouraged by the government as a means of returning to the Indians what is regarded as their original lands.[253]

---

[249] *Ibid.,* Feb. 16, 17, 18, 20, 1922.

[250] The will was probated on Oct. 17, 1923. The ranch included 4,701 hectares or 11,611 acres. Anna Sutter Young and Cristina Sutter van Wolbeck each received one-fourth; another fourth went to the three daughters of Sofía; an eighth went to Juan Norbert and another eighth to his daughter, Dolores Sutter Kason. ("Claim for Expropriation of Property in Mexico," Aug. 19, 1942, in Sutter, Jr., Papers.)

[251] In 1915 Mrs. Anna Sutter Young and her husband spent some $10,000 in Mexico rebuilding the rancho, but violence broke out and forced their withdrawal. In the following year Juan Norbert and a man named Lombardi are reported to have spent $15,000 on the property, but their work was destroyed and they, too, were forced off.

[252] Statement by Mrs. Young.

[253] On Aug. 19, 1942, the dispossessed heirs drew up before a San Francisco notary public a claim by which they hope, through the American State Dept., to receive indemnity for their lost property. The claim includes $47,010 for 4,701 hectares of land, $42,200 for permanent improvements on the rancho, $60,000

Nicolasa Sutter's effort in 1915–1916 to regain the Sacramento property, which the city had allegedly used in violation of the original terms of her husband's gift, was not the only such attempt. Since 1873 the city of Sacramento, large corporations, various Sutter heirs, and other individuals have fought again and again in the courts of California over real or supposed rights.[254]

But in all cases involving the right of Sacramento city to the property, the city has been triumphant. Today, green parks, playing fields, and public buildings occupy those well placed blocks, all because John Sutter, Jr., though exposed to the fever of the greatest gold-madness this country has ever experienced, retained a vision of the public good. Out of his early visit to Washington, D. C., on his way from Europe, came the memory of a geometrically planned city. Today, young Sutter's California capital, its central district evenly platted on thirty-one numbered and twenty-four lettered streets, amply dotted by shady parks, stands as the metropolis of the great valley in which his father pioneered.

---

for crops lost over a period of twelve years, and $1,510 for livestock: a total of $150,780 in American money.

[254] For additional information see Appendix II.

Part II: *Statement Regarding Early California Experiences, by John A. Sutter, Jr.*

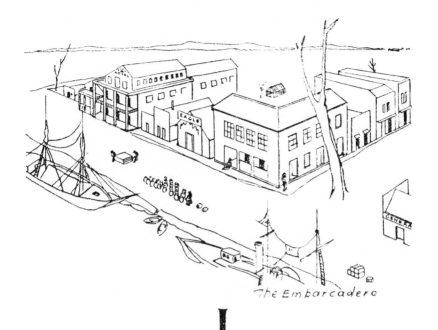

The Embarcadero

I ARRIVED IN CALIFORNIA IN THE
MONTH OF AUGUST, 1848;[1] THE GOLD HAD BEEN DISCOVERED ONLY
A FEW WEEKS PREVIOUSLY.[2] ALREADY IN SAN FRANCISCO I HEARD
some very strange reports and altogether contradictory rumors about
my father and the state of his affairs.

Some said he was the richest man on earth and did not know himself his wealth; others in the contrary told me in confidence that my
father on account of his dreadfully loose and careless way of doing
every business transaction was on the brink of ruin and that instead
of having in his employ good and trustworthy men, he was surrounded by a parcel of rogues and immoral men, which, instead of helping
him, only would accelerate and in a short period accomplish his utter

---

[1] Sutter, Jr., arrived at San Francisco on Sept. 14, 1848, aboard the ship *Huntress.* "Among the passengers by the *Huntress,* from New York, we notice Capt.
Rufus Ingalls, of the Quarter Master's Department, Lieut. Norton, 1st Regt. N.Y.
Volunteers, recently disbanded, and Mr. J. A. Sutter, Jr., son of the enterprising
proprietor of New Helvetia." (*Californian,* Sept. 16, 1848.)

[2] Gold was discovered on Jan. 19 or 24, the later date being the one generally
accepted.

moral, physical, and financial ruin. Some even went further; the very
first day I was on shore at San Francisco, they came to me request-
ing me to interfere energetically in the business of my father, to chase
all those men in his employ away, to replace them by other good ones
and to attend to all the business myself in person, if I wanted to save
something yet for my mother, brothers, for my father himself and
for me. Some even presented to me their claims against him, telling
me how long they had been waiting and waited yet for payment
and expected now from me, that I would cause them to be paid as
soon as possible. My father's agent in San Francisco at the time was
Mr. Petter Sherrebeck,[3] a Dane, who, I think, at present is living in
San Jose; I then already had a chance to judge for myself of the way
my father's business was attended to. It is impossible for anybody to
imagine with what contradictory feelings I set out for Sacramento,
the next day after my arrival at San Francisco in the schooner[4] of my
father, which had happened to be there. All these contradictory reports had made a dreadful impression upon my mind. Having never
before heard that my father was affected with the dreadful vice of
drinking and other disorderly habits, I really could and would not
believe it until further proof. Arriving at Sacramento the first people
I met with, were Mr. George McDougall's[5] clerks and men on board

---

[3] Peter Sherreback, a Dane who arrived in San Francisco in 1840, became a
trader there and was active in early civil affairs, serving as collector and on the
town council. (Bancroft, *Calif.,* V, 719.)

[4] This was the schooner *Sacramento,* acquired from the Russians when Sutter,
Sr., purchased their Fort Ross-Bodega properties in 1841. It was used largely on
the New Helvetia-Yerba Buena run, captained by a white master and manned
by an Indian crew. (*Sacramento Union,* July 25, 1860.) Her tonnage has been
variously estimated at from seventeen to forty tons.

[5] George McDougal, who became one of young Sutter's most formidable opponents, was an Ohioan who came overland to California in 1845. For a time he
worked in the redwoods near Santa Cruz, then lived in Gilroy, where he led a
carefree life. A constant search for an easy way of making a living was a charac-
teristic of his entire life. In the Mexican War he accompanied Frémont on his
southern California campaign. In 1847-48 he was a gambler and speculator in
town lots in San Francisco. Shortly after the gold discovery at Coloma, McDougal
formed a partnership, towed a hulk load of goods up the river, and set up shop
on the *Embarcadero* near what is now the foot of K Street, where, declared one
of his clerks, "they made stacks of money." (McChristian, *Narrative,* ms.) About
1853 McDougal began a roving life, living among the Indians of the Southwest,
and was rarely seen. In 1867 he was discovered in Patagonia, where, as "king"

his vessel, Robert Ridley,[6] (now dead) a German by the name of Hahn,[7] an American, Lang,[8] which latter three were pointed out to me as my father's business men. Ridley was sick and two days afterwards went to San Francisco. I never saw him again. Hahn and Lang, I saw drunk the first day I was at the fort. My father had gone to the mines and was only expected to be back in some days, so that I was left alone with my reflections about the rumors I had heard in San Francisco and moreover everything not only was confirmed but painted to me in stronger and more vivid colors than ever before.

I saw myself how everything went on. Anything belonging to my father was at everybody's disposal. The traders in the fort, (Brannan,[9]

---

of a tribe of Indians, he was trying to develop a gold mine. He committed suicide in Washington in 1872. (Bancroft, *Calif.*, IV, 723; VI, 645–646; *Themis*, Mar. 3, 1889; Winfield J. Davis, "Stormy Life of 'Lord' George M'Dougal," *Sacramento Union*, Sept. 13, 1901.) W. F. Swasey, who was in the same overland company, says that he was "exceedingly gentle and captivating in his manner," and "from 1845 to 1849 no man was more universally and favorably known in California." (*Early days*, p. 179.)

[6] Robert Ridley, an English sailor, was for some years employed by August's father as captain of the *Sacramento* and as manager of the Fort Ross property. In 1848 he became *alcalde* at the San Francisco Mission. (Bancroft, *Calif.*, V, 695.)

[7] The identity of this man is uncertain. A Matthew J. Haan arrived in California in 1846 from Honolulu and became a trader at Sonoma. (Bancroft, *Calif.*, III, 773.) In the *New Helvetia Diary*, Sutter wrote on May 13, 1848, that Mr. Haan had left for the mountains. Swasey (*Early Days*, pp. 35, 271) gives as a member of the Swasey-Todd party of 1845 a Francis Hoen, whom Bancroft declares to have been for a time in Captain Sutter's employ. (*Calif.*, III, 786.) One Kaan is also mentioned by Bancroft as being at New Helvetia in 1848. (*Calif.*, IV, 696.)

[8] This was Charles Lang, who arrived in California in 1848 from Boston on the *Sabine*. (Bancroft, *Calif.*, IV, 705.) According to Lienhard, who had no respect for him, he was the only son of a rich Boston father who had spared no expense in giving the boy a good education. Lang became one of the rowdies about the Fort and quite disgusted Lienhard with his vulgar remarks about Captain Sutter. When August met him he was a member of a volunteer bodyguard for Sutter, who was fearful of being robbed. (Lienhard, *Pioneer*, p. 165.) Several years later Lang had become so shabby and emaciated that Lienhard was astounded at this "example of depravity and its consequences." (*Memoiren*, ms., fol. 144.)

[9] Samuel Brannan, a Maine printer born at Saco in 1819, led a large colony of Mormon Saints to California by sea in 1846. In 1847 he organized the firm of C. C. Smith & Co., soon changed to Brannan & Co., with a store in Sutter's Fort, supplying goods to the new settlers in the valley. His profits were enormous and laid the foundation for the greatest fortune in early day California. (Bancroft, *Calif.*, II, 728.) In 1849 he purchased from Sutter, Jr., four square miles of land

Ellis,[10] Pettit,[11] Dr. McKie,[12] Capt. Dring,[13] Pickett,[14] a.s.f.) furnished anybody who wanted it, with enormous bills for my father's
account. Indians, Negroes, Kanakas and white men of any nation in-
discriminately by applying to my father, easily obtained letters of
credit from him to any amount for any stores existing then in or
about the fort. Every man in his employ of course wanted to acquire
my confidence and friendship; everyone told me a different tale, each
more or less dreadful accounts, in the same time calumniating one
another. At that time arrived at the fort also Major Hensley[15] and

on the west side of the Feather River where he developed a ranch. (*U. S.* v. *Sutter*, pp. 294–295, 804, 839.) Brannan may have been no worse than many men of
his time who, by fair means and foul, sought riches in the new country. Perhaps
the kindest description of him in his business dealings would be that he was a
cunning opportunist.

[10] "Genial, whole-souled, smiling, rolicking, open-handed, open-hearted Alf
Ellis" had a store at the Fort in Sept., 1848, where he was rapidly accumulating
a fortune. (*Alta Calif.*, Aug. 3, 1866.) He arrived in California from the Hawaiian Islands in 1847, opened a saloon and boarding house in Yerba Buena before
the gold rush, went to Sutter's Fort, but soon returned to San Francisco where he
became quite prominent. He helped to organize the First California Guard, served
on the town council, and was elected to the Assembly in 1851. Ellis Street in San
Francisco was named for him. (Bancroft, *Calif.*, II, 790; V, 684; *San Francisco
Examiner*, July 29, 1883; *Call*, July 30, 1883.)

[11] A Huber Petit or Pettit came to California in 1846 and in 1847 was sheriff
at New Helvetia. (Bancroft, *Calif.*, IV, 775; *New Helvetia Diary*, pp. 98, 99.)
Prominent in early Sacramento was an A. P. Petit or Pettit. He advertised as a
contractor and builder in Dec., 1849 (*Placer Times*, Dec. 29, 1849) and was
elected a councilman in 1850. (Colville, *Sacramento Directory, 1853–54.*) He
built the first Sacramento County court house in 1850 (*Sacramento Transcript*,
June 21, 1850) and owned a brick-making yard in Sutterville. (*Sacramento
Union*, Feb. 18, Apr. 24, 1853.)

[12] Dr. William H. McKee, a Scotch physician living in Monterey about 1846,
who later opened a store in Sutter's Fort. (Bancroft, *Calif.*, IV, 724; Bryant,
What I Saw in Calif., p. 299.)

[13] Captain David Dring, master of the Hudson's Bay Co. bark *Janet*, left the
Columbia River for California June 8, 1848. (*Oregon Spectator*, June 15, 1848,
quoted in *Oregon Hist. Quarterly*, XL [1939], 170.) He opened a store in Sutter's Fort and continued to operate there even after most of the merchants had
moved down near the river, for on Apr. 21, 1849, he paid $5,000 to Hensley,
Reading & Co. for part of the southeast corner of the Fort. (Sacramento County,
Deed Books, vol. A, pp. 682–684.)

[14] Charles E. "Philosopher" Pickett was a lawyer of eccentric character. He
wrote for the newspapers and was the author of many political and social pamph-
lets advocating some reform or abusing someone. (Bancroft, *Calif.*, IV, 776; VI,
454; Powell, *Philosopher Pickett.*)

[15] Major Samuel Hensley, an overland arrival of 1843, was for some time in

Mr. McKinstry;[16] the former I had known already in Washington
City; both had been in the employ of my father formerly and were
well acquainted with his affairs as a matter of course. Both these gentlemen told to me the same as anybody else and further informed me,
that my father owed to the American Russian fur company of the
North West coast the amount of $30,000 with interests, resulting from
the acquisition of Bodega and Ross,[17] that Mr. Leidesdorff, the agent
of said company had sued my father for this amount and that the
sheriff of San Francisco has levied an attachment on the whole property of my father.[18] (Mr. McKinstry is well acquainted with these

---

the elder Sutter's employ, first as supercargo of the river launch, then as com-
missary in Sutter's campaign with Micheltorena. He was later majordomo of
Hock Farm and acquired an intimate knowledge of his employer's affairs. Young
Sutter first met him in the East, where he testified at Frémont's court-martial. In
the fall of 1848 he organized the firm of Hensley, Reading & Co. He later became
interested in river steamers and was the second president of the California Steam
Navigation Co. He died near San Jose in 1866, at the age of forty-nine. He was
probably one of the most respected men in early California. (Bancroft, *Calif.*, III,
781; Historical Records Survey, *Calendar Major Jacob Rink Snyder Collection*,
p. 40; *Alta Calif.*, Jan. 9, 1866.)

[16] George McKinstry, Jr., was prominent for a time in early affairs at Sutter's
Fort and Sacramento. Born in New York state, he came overland in 1846, and for
the next five years lived at the Fort and at Sutterville. In 1847 he became the
majordomo of New Helvetia. He was the first sheriff of the Sacramento district
and was active in the relief of the ill-fated Donner party. Some time later he
moved to southern California and in 1867 was listed as a physician at Old Town,
San Diego. (McKinstry, letter in the *First Annual Meeting and Banquet, Associated Pioneers of the Territorial Days of Calif.*, pp. 77–78; Bancroft, *Calif.*, IV,
725; Black, *San Diego County*, I, 218.)

[17] Sutter made the purchase on Dec. 13, 1841, for $30,000, to be paid in an-
nual installments, partly in grain and partly in cash. Sutter, Jr., later settled this
account. (*Supra*, pp. 27–28.)

[18] In 1846 when there seemed a possibility that Captain Sutter might sell New
Helvetia to the United States for $80,000, William Alexander Leidesdorff, who
had just been appointed agent of the Russians, levied an attachment against the
Sutter holdings to safeguard the unpaid debt to the fur company. Leidesdorff,
son of a Danish father and a negro mother, was born in the Danish West Indies
and first arrived in California as a shipmaster in 1841. Settling in San Francisco,
he became an outstanding citizen and held several civil offices. In 1844 he was
granted a rancho on the American River next to Sutter's New Helvetia, and the
following year became U. S. vice-consul in San Francisco. He was friendly to
Sutter, who in 1845 owed him over $1,000, and did his best to satisfy the Russian
demands without actually foreclosing. He died in the May previous to August's
arrival. (Bancroft, *Calif.*, IV, 711; VI, 192–193; Zollinger, *Sutter*, pp. 163, 204,
219.)

facts).[19] Major Hensley then went away to Major Reading's[20] place, having heard that this gentleman was very dangerously ill from the consequences of an accidental shot. Mr. McKinstry stayed with me in order to urge my father to transfer all his real estate as well as personal property to me, Major Hensley and him having come to the conclusion that this was the only way to stop the execution of the attachment, until there could be procured means to pay this debt, as well as all others which they estimated to be after their best kno[w]ledge about $80,000. From the books I received from Hahn, I never could obtain any kno[w]ledge of the state of affairs on account of their dreadful confusion; also they had been neglected for about six months. As a proof of the confusion of things, I only will state that I found the now so important original map of Capt. Vioget[21] in an open drawer, as also the contract with the Russian American company and ackno[w]ledged bills and accounts of Col. Fremont.

At last after a week of terrible excitement and anguish, my father, whom I had not seen for fifteen years, arrived. Our first meeting after such a long separation was as affectionate and sincere as ever meeting ought to be between father and son on such an occasion. We wept both. Seeing my father so kind, so affectionate, I soon forgot all I had heard and was as happy of having met with him as I could

---

[19] *Supra*, pp. 11–12.

[20] Major Pierson B. Reading, one of the most respected men of pioneer times, arrived in California in 1843, went to work for Captain Sutter, was active in the American conquest of California, and in 1849 went into business with Samuel Hensley, Jacob Snyder, and Sutter, Jr. He was a candidate for governor in 1851 and was said to have been defeated because his friendship with Sutter cost him the squatter votes. He later took up farming on his Shasta County rancho and died in 1868 at the age of fifty-two. (Bancroft, *Calif.*, V, 689; Dana, *Sutter of Calif.*, p. 373.)

[21] This was the official map of the Sutter grant. It was a sketch survey made for Sutter by Captain Jean Jacques Vioget in 1841. Unfortunately Vioget's instruments were faulty, and his map showed the southern boundary, several miles south of the present site of Sacramento, to be 38° 49' 32" north latitude. This was to cause considerable dispute when it was later determined that this latitude ran north of the city. Squatters found the discrepancy most convenient. (Bancroft, *Calif.*, IV, 229–231; Zollinger, *Sutter*, p. 301; *U. S.* v. *Sutter*, pp. 70, 548.) Vioget was a Swiss mariner and surveyor who first came to California in 1837 and was master of several vessels in the coast trade before settling in San Francisco to run a billiard saloon and hotel. He was one of Sutter's two witnesses at the purchase of the Russian property. (Bancroft, *Calif.*, IV, 179; V, 764.)

be. We spoke a long time of my mother, my brothers and sister, family matters and times long gone by; my father very often was moved to tears; then we commenced to converse on his present state of affairs; he would soothe all my fears, telling me of his plans for the time to come, of his hopes to be soon out of all difficulties, a.s.f. I was quite happy. Mr. McKinstry then came and proposed to him the plan of transferring everything to me, and my father, seeing the necessity of it, at once consented to it very readily. Two days after this there arrived at the fort Mr. Myron Norton[22] and Mr. Gilbert,[23] the former one of my fellow passengers from New York to San Francisco, who had come out to join the regiment of N. Y. Volunteers under Col. Stevenson, as a lieutenant; the other also had been an officer in the same regiment which then already was disbanded, and although lawyers, they were on their way from San Francisco to the mines. I informed my father that these gentlemen had arrived and that I knew Mr. Norton to be able to draw up an instrument for the purpose already mentioned. He consented to have it done forthwith. I went to explain to Mr. Norton my business and introduced him and his friend to my father. They went to work and two documents to the aforementioned effect were drawn up and signed by my father, one relating to the real estate, the other to all his personal property.[24]

---

[22] Norton, a lieutenant in the New York Volunteers, arrived in California with Sutter, Jr., on the *Huntress*. He was a San Francisco delegate to the Constitutional Convention. He had been a lawyer in Vermont and, in 1850, was a member of Norton, Satterlee & Norton, San Francisco law firm. Later he moved to Los Angeles and became prominent as a county judge. (Bancroft, *Calif.*, IV, 755; VI, 279, 288; Kimball, *San Francisco City Directory, 1850.*)

[23] Edward Gilbert was an able young man who arrived in California from New York in 1847 as a lieutenant in the New York Volunteers. He was a delegate to the Constitutional Convention, one of the founders and the first editor of the *Alta California,* and one of the owners of the *Placer Times.* He was a frequent Sacramento visitor and bought considerable property in the new town. He was elected California's first congressman. His promising career was cut short in a duel near Sacramento in 1852, when he was thirty-three. (Bancroft, *Calif.*, III, 756; IV, 735; VI, 288; Sacramento County, *Deed Books,* vol. A, pp. 415, 491–493, 601, 696, 713, 715.)

[24] *Supra,* p. 12. They were dated Oct. 14, 1848. The real estate was described as starting at latitude $39° 33' 45''$ on the east bank of the Sacramento River and extending to three leagues east of the Feather River, thence south to $38° 41' 32''$, west to the Sacramento, and northwesterly and north along the course of the river past the mouth of the Feather to the starting point. Excluded were a tract owned

These documents, if I am not mistaken, have been recorded afterwards in the records of Sacramento City. I knew very well that, if the country had been in a settled state of affairs, this transfer would have been of no avail whatever, an attachment on the property having been levied before; a good many people told me so at the time. It was after any laws in any country an *illegal* act. I knew it to be so at the time; the gentlemen who wrote it knew it to be so likewise; and in my opinion a large amount of property, in fact *all Sacramento City* can be saved and recovered by only obtaining proofs in regard to this matter, which will be easy if there are any old records in San Francisco. By proving that the transfer was illegal, all the property claimed under me with no exceptions whatever will fall back to my father. I am ready to give my testimony under oath, knowing it to be the perfect truth. Witnesses can be obtained easily; it was publicly known that my father's property was attached. Even the men who bought from me, I suppose, could not deny this fact on oath. This question involves an immense amount of property and will create a great excitement; however for the benefit of my family I am ready to suffer its consequences to any extent whatever. I am afraid of nothing in this respect which could keep me back from taking this step. I am convinced that some able, honest, eminent and independent lawyer, after the decision of the land commission in regard to the title,[25] going cautiously but at the same time energetically to work, will have good success in this matter and be able to save something from the general wreck for my family.

This happened in the month of Sept. or commencement of October. A few days after this my father returned to the mines and left me alone with all the confusions at the fort.

---

by Elias Grimes and parcels granted to John Smith in 1844, Michael Nye in 1844, Nicolaus Altgeier in 1840, Edward Farwell in 1844, and a half mile of land in Sutterville, conveyed to Lansford W. Hastings in 1845. The Fort Ross property, a lot in San Francisco, the sawmill, and a square mile of land at Coloma were included. (Sacramento County, *Deed Books*, vol. A, pp. 1–3; vol. C, pp. 351–353; reprinted in *U. S. v. Sutter*, pp. 88–89.)

[25] The United States Land Commission confirmed Sutter's two grants on May 15, 1855. They were later brought before the United States District and Supreme courts.

Instead of gaining anything in the mines, I only say that wagon-loads of provisions of any kind, dry goods, a.s.f., bought at enormous prices were taken off by him and his agents to his camp and there each one, as many as there were, Indians, Kanakas, and white men robbed and stole what they could; very little gold I ever saw from their labour. In the contrary all the bills I had to pay afterwards with lots, money, cattle, sheep, horses or anything I could lay my hands on. All the rents of the fort, about $3,000 monthly, were always drawn upon in advance. People who up in the mines had entrusted their gold for safekeeping to my father could very often not obtain it back from him, when he then used to give to them orders on me, to pay them as well and as fast as I could. With everybody he went in partner-ship for mining purposes; he furnished provisions, Indians to do the work, a.s.f. and always his partners got the whole and sole benefit of it. All this time hardly a day passed on which he himself and his clerks, partners, Indians, etc., were not on a general frolic intoxicated as I then already had had an opportunity of seeing such things at the fort, I am sorry to say, more than once. The best time was lost in this manner. We were over head and ears in old debts and notwithstand-ing the time, when everybody who wanted to do so, acquired in a short time great wealth, I only saw new debts accumulating them-selves very rapidly and every day upon us. Our stock was not at-tended to. Whoever wanted meat killed sheep, hogs and beeves at discretion;[26] whoever had a mind to lay his hands on a horse or mule did so. Every day news from the mines arrived, worse and worse, and every day there were people calling for money and settlement of their accounts. I am sure there was not a man in the fort or in San Fran-cisco, not a man, I may say so, in the country, with whom my father had not unsettled accounts, and of course everybody said they had claims *against* him. I knew that the launch on the river made every trip a large sum of money; though the proceeds of this and of a ferry-boat which was established on the river just this side the slough, all

---

[26] Captain Sutter recalled later that one of his sons, riding after stock at Hock Farm, discovered a man ruthlessly butchering a fine imported Durham cow val-ued at $300. ("General Sutter's Diary," *Argonaut,* Feb. 16, 1878, p. 7.)

remained in the hands of Mr. George McDougall for goods furnished to my father at extravagant prices.

At the same time I knew that my mother and my brothers were anxiously waiting in Europe, and I can assure you not in brilliant circumstances, for me to send to them news from my father and from me, as also pecuniary aid. I knew well they depended upon me to send them the means to come here.

What favorable news, what consolation could I send to my poor mother as a compensation of so many years toiling and sufferings? I beg everybody to take all these circumstances in consideration, and although I by no means want to wash myself clear of a great many faults I have committed on account of the terrible state of feverish excitement I sometimes arrived at, I hope also in the same time that they will mitigate my behavior in a great many instances in the eyes of impartial judges.

About that time Mr. Henry Schoolcraft[27] arrived at the fort; he offered to me his services in arranging our books and I engaged him at once for this purpose. The late and so much regretted Capt. Warner[28] of the topographical engineers, who afterwards was killed by the Indians, arrived at the fort in some business of Gov. Mason.[29] Mr. Brannan and others had suggested to me already before the propriety of having the fort and the surrounding plain until to the river laid out in a city and introduced to me Capt. Warner as the

---

[27] Henry A. Schoolcraft, a sergeant in the New York Volunteers, arrived in California in 1847. Shortly after being hired by young Sutter he became, in the spring of 1849, first *alcalde* of Sacramento. He went east, secured appointment as port collector for Sacramento, but died on his way back in 1853 near Acapulco. (Bancroft, *Calif.,* V, 713; VI, 455.)

[28] Captain William H. Warner arrived in California with General Kearny in 1846. On Sept. 26, 1849, while returning from an expedition to discover a suitable railway pass over the Sierra, he was killed by Indians near Goose Lake. (Bancroft, *Calif.,* V, 768; Stoddard, "William H. Warner," *Engineerogram,* I [1939], 3–4.)

[29] Colonel Richard B. Mason on May 31, 1847, succeeded General Kearny as military governor of California, serving until Feb., 1849, when he was relieved by General Persifer F. Smith. It was Mason who despatched Lieutenant Loeser to Washington with documents and a caddy of gold confirming the gold discovery in California. (Bancroft, *Calif.,* IV, 734; VI, 115–116.) Zollinger declares that it was Mason who pressed Sutter for payment of the Russian debt. (*Sutter,* pp. 274–275.)

best man to make the survey. Squatters already then wanted to intrude upon our rights at the embarcadero and I saw that it was necessary to do something, a great many people wanting locations for stores, boarding houses, a.s.f. I engaged therefore Capt. Warner, who had obtained a leave of absence, and I am ready to say that he always proved to me a true friend and a gentleman in every respect of the word. As soon as he had commenced his work, everybody commenced to buy lots at the river at $500 a piece and in the vicinity of the fort at $250. Mr. George McDougall at this time wanted to get the whole waterfront for himself for some paltry consideration, threatening me that if I should not accede to his proposal, he should establish a preemption claim to the land.

Having consulted with Capt. Warner and others I did not accede to it, and then Mr. McDougall, all his party, the men Hahn and Lang, I had driven away, Mssrs. Hastings,[30] Cheever,[31] Gordon[32] and many

---

[30] Lansford Warren Hastings was born in Ohio in 1819 and at twenty-three led an immigrant party to Oregon. The next year he arrived in California, where he had hopes of setting up a Pacific republic, presumably with himself as its head. Realizing his plans were premature, he returned east, hoping, by lectures and the publication of his *Emigrant's Guide*, to attract sufficient settlers to California for his purpose. He and Bidwell laid out the town of Sutterville. He then served as captain in the California Battalion in the Mexican War. As secular agent of the Mormon Church, he tried to establish a town at Montezuma. He was a lawyer in San Francisco, specializing on land titles, and served as a Sacramento delegate to the Constitutional Convention in 1849. In the late 1850's he moved to Arizona, and during the Civil War he had grandiose schemes for bringing it into the Confederacy. He died a few years later on the way to Brazil. Bancroft describes him as "never without some grand scheme on hand, not overburdened with conscientious scruples, but never getting caught in anything very disreputable." (Bancroft, *Calif.*, III, 778–779; Hunsaker, "Lansford Warren Hastings, Empire Dreamer and California Pioneer," *Grizzly Bear Magazine*, XLVII [1930], 14–15, 68–71.)

[31] Henry Chever, born in Massachusetts, first came to California in 1846 as a shipmaster. He was a member of early Los Angeles trading firms and later of Sutter, Hastings & Co. at Coloma in 1849. He became active in Sacramento efforts to establish a civil government, and in 1849 was one of the founders of Yuba City. He died in the Napa Valley in 1854. (Bancroft, *Calif.*, II, 758; V, 578; VI, 455, 488; Edward E. Chever, "First Settlement of Yuba City," in Soc. Calif. Pioneers, *Quarterly*, IX [1932], 4, 227.)

[32] Robert Gordon arrived in California in 1846 from Honolulu, and the next year was editor for a short time of the *Californian*. On Jan. 8, 1849, he served as temporary secretary of the second meeting held in Sacramento to consider a provisional government for California. In the fall he was living with Chever in Coloma. He became a merchant in 1853 in Auburn, where he built the first brick

more conceived the plan to sow discord between father and son, informing him of what I had done in an unfavorable light, misrepresenting everything and calumniating me in every way possible. They touched him very readily to the quick, being well acquainted with his disposition (a great advantage they had over me who had not seen my father since the age of eight years), telling him it was an act of irreverence towards him I had committed in selling pieces of the fort and in not forwarding the interests of Sutterville which bore his name and in changing the name of "Nueva Helvetia" in "Sacramento City."

The fort, an adobe building very much neglected with leaking roofs, was about falling to pieces in its dilapidated state, and certainly only the scarcity and enormous price of lumber (one dollar pr foot) and the impossibility of finding carpenters even at the highest wages could induce people to buy it. I think we realized out of it nearly 40,000$. What would we have got for it afterwards?

The attention of everybody was drawn upon this place and not upon Sutterville; even if I had wanted to do so, I could not have stemmed the current. Nobody would go to Sutterville and if I had not commenced selling lots at Sacramento, everybody would have gone to squatting. The name of Sacramento City was proposed to me by Capt. Warner, Mr. Brannan and a great many others and I think that even today a good many people will agree with me that it is a more proper name than "Nueva Helvetia."

Judge Burnett[33] arrived about in the beginning of December at the

---

store, and served as postmaster of the town from Feb. 2, 1856, to Apr. 10, 1861. On Jan. 8, 1877, he shot himself because of alleged financial difficulties. He was quite respected in Auburn for his honesty and liberality. (Bancroft, *Calif.*, III, 762; Sioli, *Historical Souvenir of Eldorado County*, p. 179; *Alta Calif.*, Jan. 25, 1849, Jan. 9, 12, 1877; Ambrose O'Connell, First Assistant Postmaster General, to the writer, Nov. 25, 1941.)

[33] Born in Tennessee in 1807, Burnett travelled overland to Oregon in 1843, became a farmer, legislator, and territorial Supreme Court judge. The discovery of gold drew him to the Yuba River mines, but after a month of mining he continued south to Sutter's Fort. Becoming young Sutter's agent, he acquired considerable property, one-half of which he sold for $50,000. He became a judge of the California Supreme Court, and in 1849 was elected the state's first civil governor. He resigned in 1851 to attend to private business. He served a second term on the Supreme Court, was president of the Pacific Bank and built up a consider-

fort,[34] and as I was entirely ignorant of the business which was to be attended to in my new sphere, I confess it openly, and as I needed then a lawyer in my employ, to arrange matters, I engaged Mr. Burnett, having been advised by Major Reading, Major Hensley, Mr. James King of Wm.[35] to do so by all means. These gentlemen told me Judge Burnett was a man of a highly respectable character. Judge Burnett was to arrange all our business, settle all accounts, defend me in law suits, draw up all the documents in such cases, write all the deeds conveying property, bonds for such, in fact to attend to all and every business which should happen to turn up and to receive as a salary the fourth part of all the proceeds of sales of town lots of Sacramento City. I did it not without reflection and only after a long conversation with Major Reading and Mr. King. I consider it yet the best thing I could have done under the circumstances. Mr. King, as also Major Reading, always was an open, frank and independent man, who knew my affairs perfectly well and I am sure they gave me their candid advice on the matter. Mr. King is too proud not to express his opinion in any affair.

My father had then removed to the sawmill, Coloma, where he had entered into partnership with Mssrs. Hastings, Cheever and Gordon. There they lived on for several months in the accustomed manner. All at once there was raised by these insatiable leeches of my father a general outcry against Judge Burnett and against me; also by all the parties interested in Sutterville we were execrated, although I made to them the fair proposition to exchange their property in that place

able fortune. (Burnett, *Recollections*, pp. 294, 296, 341; Bancroft, *Calif.*, II, 736–737.)

[34] Burnett says he arrived at the Fort on Dec. 21, 1848. (*Recollections*, p. 272.) He was hired by Sutter, Jr., on Dec. 30. (Sacramento County, *Deed Books*, vol. A, p. 40.)

[35] Born in Georgetown, D. C., in 1822, King came to California in 1848 and became a bookkeeper for Hensley, Reading & Co. On Mar. 2, 1849, he purchased a considerable tract of Sacramento waterfront from Sutter, Jr. On Jan. 1, 1850, he and Jacob R. Snyder opened a banking business in Sacramento which was discontinued on Mar. 5, 1852. King later founded the San Francisco *Bulletin* and his vitriolic attacks on gambling and corruption resulted in his murder on May 14, 1856 and led to the formation of the second Vigilance Committee. (Bancroft, *Popular Tribunals*, II, 22–695; Colville, *Sacramento Directory, 1853–54*, p. 1; *Placer Times*, Dec. 29, 1849.)

for lots in Sacramento City. Some of them accepted. Mr. Hastings used to say at that time openly and in presence of my father, without being esteemed any less for it, he wanted to kill me. Judge Burnett, of course, soon was in the eyes of my father, before they ever had had an interview, a hypocrite, a jesuit, a designing swindler, a.s.f. My father unhappily never changed his prejudicial opinion which had been forced upon him. I have the firm belief that if Judge Burnett could have been retained for the management of our affairs up to the present date, my father would be now one of the richest men in California.

In December already, I think, I received a letter from Commodore Persifer Smith,[36] informing me that he had received instructions from Washington to settle the claim of the Russian American Fur Company, the said company having complained through the medium of the Russian minister to government of the impossibility of collecting any payment from my father and of there not existing then any courts of justice in the country. Judge Burnett immediately answered stating our readiness to make the full payment and in the month of January arrived at the fort Col. Stuart, U.S.A., for the purpose of receiving the payment.[37] We gave him, I think, some $10,000 in gold dust and the rest in notes which we had received for town lots and which were collected afterwards by the agents of the company. We settled the same month a claim amounting to some $7,000 of the Hudson's Bay

---

[36] General Persifer F. Smith arrived in California aboard the steamer *California*, Feb. 26, 1849, as commander of the Pacific Division and succeeding Governor Mason. Bancroft calls Smith a blunderer in civil affairs. (Bancroft, *Calif.*, VI, 272–274.)

[37] William M. Steuart (usually spelled Stewart) arrived in California in 1848 as secretary to Commodore Thomas ap Catesby Jones. In San Francisco he served on the council, was a justice of the peace, and was one of the city's delegates to the Constitutional Convention. Sometime in 1848 or 1849 he became the agent of the Russians. Zollinger declares that after Steuart received the money he promptly vanished. (*Sutter*, pp. 264–265, 275.) He, however, remained in San Francisco for a time. Burnett says he paid Steuart on Apr. 13, 1849. (Burnett to Sutter, Jr., Jan. 18, 1894, in Sutter, Jr. Papers.) On June 17 Steuart presided at a meeting in San Francisco (Bancroft, *Calif.*, VI, 278) and on Sept. 3 was at the Constitutional Convention. (Bancroft, *Calif.*, VI, 287–288.) During October and November he was campaigning for the governorship. (Taylor, *Eldorado*, I, 221; *Calif. Blue Book, 1911*, p. 416.) He was still at San Francisco in 1854. (Bancroft, *Calif.*, V, 734.)

Company with a Mr. Douglas,[38] who had come on purpose, a claim of Mr. French[39] on the Sandwich Islands of $3,000 with Mssrs. Starkey, Janion & Co.,[40] another claim of about the same amount with Mr. Señol,[41] a gentleman of San Jose, and an infinity of other more or less important claims.

Even debts my father had contracted many years ago in Missouri, I had to pay here.

A great deal of real estate always went away to settle the debts of my father in the different stores. I think Mr. Brannan's bills alone must have amounted to about $15,000. Some merchants had used various times the same contemptible means to sell bad goods to my father at irreasonable prices on a small scale, as Mr. McDougall and others made use of some time later on a grand scale for their own purposes.

At the same time my mother wrote to me a letter, demanding urgently funds for the greatest emergencies, and I had none to send to her. Judge Burnett told me on my mentioning it to him that it was my duty to pay off every debt of my father's before sending anything to Europe, and that it would cause general dissatisfaction and furnish my enemies with a subject of further calumnies if it should be made

---

[38] Perhaps Sir James Douglas, chief of the Hudson's Bay Co. in the Northwest.

[39] William French was an American merchant at Honolulu who traded with the California mainland. It was he who in 1839 chartered the brig *Clementine,* on which the elder Sutter sailed as supercargo to California, and he furnished much of the material for the founding of New Helvetia. (Zollinger, *Sutter,* pp. 46–47; Bancroft, *Calif.,* III, 749.) Burnett writes that French "under my advice took City lots in payment of his claim" (Burnett to Sutter, Jr., Jan. 18, 1894, in Sutter, Jr., Papers), and the records show that August, on July 18, 1849, transferred to French through George S. Kenway fifty Sacramento lots valued at $10,000. (Sacramento County, *Deed Books,* vol. A, pp. 82–83.)

[40] Starkey, Janion & Co. were commission merchants in San Francisco from 1847 to 1850. Both were Englishmen, Starkey arriving in 1848 and Janion in 1847. (Bancroft, *Calif.,* IV, 691; V, 678; Kimball, *San Francisco City Directory, 1850.*)

[41] Antonio María Suñol, a native Spaniard who had resided in California since 1818 and was owner of the Rancho San José del Valle, was of great assistance to the elder Sutter in founding New Helvetia. Suñol did Sutter many services besides selling him on credit at least a thousand head of cattle, for which he had great difficulty in collecting his money. (Bancroft, *Calif.,* IV, 134, 237; V, 738; also numerous letters to Suñol in the Sutter Collection.) It was not until 1849 that Suñol was finally paid. (*Supra,* p. 30.)

known that I had remitted funds to Europe before settling all claims here. With a despairing and heavy heart I postponed that duty to some other time, seeing the correctness of the judge's remarks at once.

At the end of January my father came down from the sawmill; he would see neither me nor Judge Burnett and went to stay with Mr. McDougall and his friends. They took him down to San Francisco and made him sign, after having made him intoxicated, a bond for $40,000,[42] by which he obliged himself to obtain from me a deed in their favor for one square mile of land adjoining Sutterville, for no consideration whatever. It was then publicly known that these scoundrels had obtained the said document by this mean, nefarious and rascally contrivance. Mssrs. McKinstry, Cordua,[43] Blackburn from Santa Clara[44] joined now against me with the McDougalls and wanted to induce people to remove and settle at Sutterville, where they had removed to themselves. The McDougall deed I afterwards signed, although Judge Burnett had advised me not to pay any attention to such impudence. What could I do? I had to sign, in order to annul the bond my father had given to them.[45]

In February and March I removed everything to Hock Farm, con-

---

[42] The Sutter-McDougal agreement of Mar. 6, 1849 (in Sutter Collection), states that the bond was for $20,000.

[43] Theodore Cordua was a jolly, fat German trader of Spanish descent who came from Honolulu to California in 1842. Exchanging with Sutter $8,000 worth of goods for cattle, horses and a square mile of land on the present site of Marysville, he established there a tiny settlement known as New Mecklenburg, later as Cordua's Rancho. In 1844 he became a Mexican citizen and was given the seven-league Honcut Rancho adjoining New Mecklenburg. Selling his land for $30,000 at the beginning of the gold rush, he took to storekeeping in the mines, where he lost his money. He later returned to the Hawaiian Islands and died there. (Bancroft, *Calif.,* II, 767; IV, 671; VI, 16, 463; Zollinger, *Sutter,* pp. 111, 123.)

[44] William Blackburn came to California in 1845 with the Swasey-Todd party, opened a sawmill in partnership with George McDougal at Santa Cruz, served in the California Battalion during the Mexican War, and on returning to Santa Cruz was appointed *alcalde*. His decisions are remembered for their amusing irregularity marked with common sense and justice. He was a member of the Constitutional Convention. For a time he was a partner of McDougal in business at Sacramento and Sutterville, but returned to Santa Cruz where he became a large property holder and progressive farmer. He died in San Francisco in 1867, aged fifty-eight. (Bancroft, *Calif.,* II, 721; Swasey, *Early Days,* pp. 180–181; *Alta Calif.,* Mar. 26, 1867.)

[45] Sutter, Jr., transferred a half square mile of land to George McDougal on June 19, 1849. (Sacramento County, *Deed Books,* vol. A, pp. 116–117.)

sidering it to be a safer place for our stock. I sent up provisions, farming utensils, goods for the Indians, furniture, hogs, sheep, chicken, a.s.f., informing Mr. Richard,[46] the gentleman in charge of the place, to do his utmost for its improvement and for the comfort of the house, because I considered it already then as the future residence of the family, and as my father had expressed his wish to go to live there, I did all in my power to make Hock Farm as comfortable as the times and circumstances permitted. In April I made arrangements with Mr. Lienhardt,[47] a Swiss, to go to Europe to bring the family here, judging that their presence would influence greatly my father and detain him entirely from committing any more excesses. To do that I then had to borrow money, paying heavy percentage to Daylor[48] on the Cosumne River; but I could not wait any longer, and with great difficulties I raised some $6,000, with which amount Mr. Lienhardt set

---

[46] John Ritschard, a Bremen man, had been a captain of some sort at Naples and is said to have crossed the Atlantic in company with young Sutter. He was for a short time an overseer of slaves in Bahia, Brazil, but came to California in 1848. Sutter appointed him majordomo at Hock, while his wife had charge of the Indian girls there, teaching them housework and sewing. The Sutters placed great trust in Ritschard. In 1851 he owned the William Tell Hotel at 262 J Street, Sacramento, and his name appears as a witness on many of the records of Sutter land sales. (Bancroft, *Calif.*, V, 696; Lienhard, *Californien*, p. 267; Lienhard, *Pioneer*, pp. 192–193 and note; Culver, *Sacramento City Directory, 1851;* Chever, "Through the Straits of Magellan in 1849," in Soc. Calif. Pioneers, *Quarterly*, IV [1927], 160.)

[47] Heinrich Lienhard was born in 1822, left Europe for New Orleans in 1843, and after several years on the northern Mississippi River frontier, came overland to California in 1846. He became one of Captain Sutter's most trusted employees. After leaving California he returned to Switzerland for several years, but came back to America and was a prosperous farmer in the Middle West. A sketch of his life, by Mrs. Marguerite Eyer Wilbur, appears in Lienhard, *A Pioneer at Sutter's Fort, 1846–1850.*

[48] William Daylor, an English sailor, was said to have deserted his ship in California about 1835. He became a cook at Sutter's Fort in 1840. In 1844 he joined Jared Sheldon on his ranch on the Cosumnes River, and on Nov. 15, 1849, in partnership with W. R. Grimshaw, opened a store and Indian trading post on the rancho. Captain Sutter once had him imprisoned and sent to Monterey because of his intimacy with Sutter's favorite Kanaka girl, but he was soon released and Sutter remained in constant fear of Daylor's vengeance. In the early days of the gold rush Daylor and a companion took out $17,000 in gold within a week. He died of cholera on Oct. 30, 1850. (Lienhard, *Pioneer*, pp. 77–78; Bancroft, *Calif.*, II, 778; IV, 672; Zollinger, *Sutter*, pp. 78, 249; Davis, *Illus. Hist. Sacramento County*, p. 235.)

out on his journey on the first of June 1850. He was to receive $4,000 besides his travelling expenses as his salary.[49] In that time I one day came from Hock Farm late in the evening by the river. On my arrival at the landing place Schoolcraft came running up to me with some gentlemen, who had commenced settling in the town, in great excitement, telling me that the place was going to be ruined, that McDougall, McKinstry, Hastings, Cordua and others had all united and were making great efforts to decide all the principal merchants to remove to Sutterville by offering to them a large interest in the place, and that everybody expected from me to oppose myself to it with everything in my power and even by granting to those merchants the same advantages in Saco. City. To make the thing worse, Judge Burnett was absent; he had gone to San Francisco. I went with Mr. Schoolcraft up to the fort where I found my father with Mr. Brannan in his room. I arrived in a very excited state of mind. In the presence of my father Mr. Brannan exhibited to me a letter from Mr. McDougall by which he offered to him two hundred town lots if he should agree to remove with his house, his store ship and with his influence, then very great, to Sutterville.

He told me that similar letters had been received also by Mssrs. Hensley, Reading & Co.,[50] and by Mssrs. Priest, Lee & Co.,[51] and that it depended now upon me to ruin or to build up the place, and that they expected me to grant to them the same amount of property in Saco. City in my own interest and also for the benefit of the persons who already had invested their capital in town lots. Otherwise, he

---

[49] Lienhard left San Francisco on the steamer *Panama*, June 20, 1849. Lienhard writes that young Sutter told him he could trust only two men with the mission of bringing the family from Switzerland: Ritschard and Lienhard. August offered the latter $2,000 to undertake it, but he held out for $4,000. In addition he was to have $8,000 travelling expenses for himself and his charges, including several relatives of the Sutters. August finally agreed to the price, and Lienhard offered to take a lot at Front and O Streets in lieu of $1,000. When he returned seven months later, property had so risen in value that he was able to dispose of the lot for $10,000. (Lienhard, *Pioneer*, pp. 192–194, 209, 228.)

[50] Young Sutter was a member of this firm from Nov. 1, 1848, until May 6, 1849. (*Supra*, pp. 13–14, 24.)

[51] This firm rented a room at Sutter's Fort where they sold miners' supplies at exorbitant prices. The firm failed in the summer of 1850. (Bancroft, *Calif.*, VI, 454; Sacramento Bee, *Sacramento Guide Book*, p. 55.)

said, they were going to abandon Sacramento City. My father heard everything himself, told me he knew McDougall had made such offers to these gentleman and said: Well, if it is so, you cannot do anything else, you must let have Mr. Brannan the same advantages to induce him to stay. I do not recollect exactly the words, but I swear solemnly I recollect as if it had been yesterday that my father at that moment made no objections whatever and in the contrary agreed with me; and these gentlemen obtained, each firm, two hundred town lots with the condition not to remove and to exert themselves to their utmost for the place. I have been blamed frequently, and I know I was to blame, to have acceded to these outrageous proposals so easily, but then I considered all my interests in jeopardy, myself in danger as well as those who had invested their money, and I felt myself in honor bound to sustain them. My father was present at this interview with Mr. Brannan and made no objections, I declare it once more: because at that moment, as well as at other times when he reflected coolly and impartially upon the subject, he must have seen himself the almost self evident fact that Sacramento City had been the means of paying all his debts, and that there could be made a hundred times more out of it yet, than of Sutterville, where McDougall owned one entire mile, Hastings another half mile and himself a very small portion in proportion to all the other shareholders. Public blame now falls and always has fallen upon me, because very few people are acquainted with these facts; but who was the original cause of the opposition I had to contend with? Who was the real cause of this immense loss of property but my father in his blindness himself?

If McDougall had not obtained these lands from him by fraud, Hastings, McKinstry and a good many others as a generous gift and tokens of friendship, there never would have occurred such an event. None of these people ever had paid a dime as a consideration for these lands, whilst in Sacramento City until then every lot had been sold for money or given in payment of debts at the rate of $500 and $250. Enough of it.

At the end of May I fell sick and nearly became blind through an inflammation of my eyes; fever and ague also commenced to attack me severely. I went up to Hock Farm sick in company with my father, Mr. Peachy,[52] a gentleman who had come from San Francisco and Mr. Schoolcraft. I did not know at the time whether these gentlemen came on business or on a pleasure excursion. I then most every day had attacks of fever, and some time later I became so weak that I often fell down on the floor in a swoon and had to be carried to bed. In the afternoon of the day after our arrival I was called in my father's room where everything had been prepared; my father told me that, as I was so unwell and there was now not any more necessity of the property being in my name, he wanted me to sign a conveyance transferring back to him all the property; and that he was going to appoint Mssrs. Peachy and Schoolcraft, his agent, the former gentleman for San Francisco, the latter for Sacramento City. I felt so sick and fatigued, that I signed immediately without making any further inquiries or replies. My father left again with these gentlemen for Sacramento City, and I was left alone with my fever. I only will add that as Judge Burnett, according to his agreement with me, considered himself interested for one-fourth in the city, he also claimed a quantity of lots as his share of those lots which had been granted to Mssrs. S. Brannan, Hensley, Reading & Co. and Priest, Lee & Co. Everything with him was settled in Sacramento City by Mr. Peachy, as I understood, to the satisfaction of both parties. Judge Burnett delivered then everything in his hands relating to my father's affairs to Mr. Peachy, I believe, and since then the two newly appointed agents commenced their operations.

This is what I consider as the first great period of my life in California. All the principal and most important transactions are stated herewith, and I hope that some of the explanations may enlighten my friends, the friends of our family and the public in general, if ever this should happen to be published, in regard to the unhappy diffi-

---

[52] Archibald Peachy was a clever lawyer who became Captain Sutter's agent in 1849 but was replaced by General Albert Winn in June, 1850. He is said to have made $80,000 very quickly in Sutter's employ. He was a member of the prominent legal firm of Halleck, Peachy & Billings, and later served as assemblyman and senator in the state legislature. (Dana, *Sutter of Calif.*, p. 364; Zollinger, *Sutter*, p. 298; *Sacramento Transcript*, June 11, 1850; *Alta Calif.*, June 19, 1850; *Calif. Blue Book, 1911*, pp. 585, 592.)

culties which arose and separated and keep separate yet father and son. I also repeat once more that all the property conveyed away by me in this period can be recovered by proving the existence of the attachment I have already mentioned. And for the benefit of the family, I hope that sooner or later operations to this end may be commenced.

The two brothers McDougall[53] properly may be called the two evil spirits of my life since I came to California. Directly or indirectly they always have been working on my own ruin openly and hypocritically in secret on the ruin of the rest of the family. If I had met with true friends of us both instead of having found such men in the confidence of my father, all would have been peace and harmony between us. As it was, I sometimes certainly considered it my duty, as a sacred and natural debt I owed to my mother, to my absent brothers and sister, to defend myself, although without any experience, against those men, and, as my father thought and the public still thinks, against him in that terrible struggle in which I at last, surrounded by mortal enemies and without one true friend at my side, was obliged to succumb entirely, as will be seen in the continuation of my tale. And the same men, the same demons, not content of having ruined me, always in the same time have been at work, and are at work still without relenting and with a fair prospect before them, to accomplish soon the ruin of my father and of all our house.

I declare once more solemnly that anything I state here is the whole naked truth, as far as I recollect, and has been brought to paper by me after due reflections and in an altogether quiet state of my mind.

---

[53] George McDougal (see note 5) and his brother John. The latter, born in Ohio, came overland to California in 1848 and joined his brother in business in Sacramento. (*Supra*, pp. 23–26.) He was a member of the Constitutional Convention and ran successfully for lieutenant-governor in 1849. After the resignation of Burnett, McDougal became governor in 1851. He died at San Francisco in 1866. He was a man of social talent, of fine appearance in ruffled shirt and pantaloons, and was usually heavy with alcohol. Bancroft calls him "a gentlemanly drunkard" and charges that he was seldom fit for his official duties. Generally popular, commanding, and with an educated mind, he was a formidable opponent for young Sutter. (Bancroft, *Calif.*, IV, 723; VI, 276, 279, 288, 291, 305, 446, 644–645; Colville, *Sacramento Directory, 1853–54*, pp. 2, 3.)

San Francisco this twenty-fifth day of the month of February in
the year of Our Lord 1855.   JOHN A. SUTTER, JR.

☆

Passing without making any mention of it a space of about six
months, during which period I had been sick most of the time, living
at Hock Farm without any knowledge or interference with the business of my father, the second great period of my life in California
commences with the arrival of our family in this country in January
1850.[54] My father, some days before this event, probably afraid I
might give to my mother, my brothers and sister to[o] much information on certain matters, which I however never did, told me he
wanted me to leave Hock Farm, where I could not enjoy any good
health; he would take his measures to give me a reasonable capital to
go in business with some young men of his acquaintance; he brought
with him for this purpose Mr. Rutte[55] and Mr. Gruningen,[56] gentlemen of whose character I from report first and afterwards from personal intercourse, I could form no favorable opinion at all. I therefore
told my father at once that these gentlemen did not suit me at all.
Already some months ago I had been made acquainted through my
father, who brought him to Hock Farm, with Dr. Brandes,[57] a German
physician, who treated me in my illness. He had been highly spoken
of to me by my father and gradually, I may say, I do not know how,
he obtained a very great influence and entire control over me. I con-

---

[54] They arrived on the *Panama,* Jan. 21, 1850. (Lienhard, *Pioneer,* p. 212;
Alta Calif., Jan. 24, 1850.)

[55] A Thomas Rutte, member of the firm of Rutte & Tissot, importers at 172
Montgomery Street, San Francisco, was in Sacramento in Jan., 1850. Lienhard
spoke favorably of this firm. Rutte may have been the man of that name who was
the Swiss consul in San Francisco in 1852. (Lienhard, *Pioneer,* p. 263; *U. S. v.
Sutter,* p. 627; Parker, *San Francisco Directory, 1852–53.*) He may have been
Teofile de Rutte. (See note 56.)

[56] A Teofile de Gruningen, in partnership with other Germans including Jacob
Rippstein, Heinrich Thomen, Teofile de Rutte, and Louis Tissot, in 1850 purchased from Sutter, Sr., a thirty-six-acre triangle of land about four and a half
miles up the American River. (Sacramento County, *Deed Books,* vol. C, pp. 379–
380; vol. D, pp. 123–124.)

[57] The name of Dr. C. Brandes appears occasionally as a witness in the records
of Sacramento land sales. Little is known about him in addition to the material
in Sutter, Jr.'s *Statement.*

sidered him as my best friend, a man of education and a superior character, as also possessing a thorough kno[w]ledge of men and the world. He introduced me to the two Mssrs. Wetzlar,[58] then established at Sacramento City as merchants in company with three other partners.

The doctor used to live with them and spoke to me always of them as able businessmen who had commenced their business career in California with nothing and in his opinion were in a fair way to a large fortune. Dr. Brandes possessed my confidence and in the same time in a high degree that of my father; he of course knew the proposals which had been made to me by my father and, seeing that Mssrs. Rutte & Gruningen were not after my fancy, he commenced to recommend to me in the strongest terms the ability, activity and probity of Mssrs. Wetzlar. He told me that, if I wanted him to do so, he would

---

[58] Of all the wolves who found the Sutters tender picking, none were more voracious than the brothers Wetzlar, Germans from Hanover. Little is known about Gustavus. Julius, born in 1812, was trained in business and early established a lace factory in Leipzig, later setting up branches in Nottingham and New York. He was in the latter city when the gold fever struck the Atlantic states, and, selling out his business, he sailed for California where he arrived in 1849 and settled in Sacramento. Following the purchase of young Sutter's property, he engaged in the real estate business and in the late 1850's he also established a fire and life insurance agency. In 1869 he founded and was president of the Capital Savings Bank, and two years later helped establish a brandy distillery. He was a trustee of the Sacramento Citizens Gas Light Co., incorporated in 1872, and in 1874 became president of the new Sacramento Smelting Co., which was taken over by Wetzlar's bank after a disastrous fire in 1879. His most disastrous venture was the Sacramento Valley Sugar Co., organized in 1870. In 1871 the company erected one of the pioneer plants in the United States at Brighton, six miles east of Sacramento, but drought, army worms, grasshoppers, lack of experience, and inefficient machinery forced the company to the wall in 1875. The machinery was sold to a more successful plant at Alvarado and the stockholders lost nearly all their investment. Wetzlar died on Apr. 29, 1878, of internal hemorrhage. A laudatory obituary appeared in the *Sacramento Union:* "He was ranked as a successful and good business man, of liberal impulses. He was of retiring habit, not given to many words, was of kindly disposition and strong domestic attachments. He was one of the men who seemed fitted by nature for pioneer eras and pioneer enterprises, having those qualities of business courage and endurance which are so necessary to successful advances in a new country." (*Sacramento Union,* May 1, 1878, reprinted in the San Jose *Pioneer,* May 11, 1878; Rolph, *Something about Sugar,* pp. 151, 153; Davis, *Illus. Hist. Sacramento County,* pp. 143, 167; Thompson and West, *Hist. Sacramento County,* pp. 148, 156; *Democratic State Journal,* supplement, Dec. 22, 1852.)

speak to them about an association with me which would be of great benefit to me in his opinion. Mssrs. Wetzlar soon came and told me that it was not an easy thing for them to break their contract with their present partners in order to enter in a new partnership with me, that, however, they would try to do so if I should bind myself to bring a capital of $30,000 to the firm.

I told them to see (with Dr. Brandes) my father, [and] that I was willing to comply with this condition if my father should be able to raise this amount of money in a given time. They went and had an interview with him on the subject. My father, taking it to be an easy thing, promised to them to procure for me until the first of March 1850 the already mentioned amount of capital. Mssrs. Wetzlar then agreed to make the *sacrifice*, as they called it, and commenced to settle their affairs with their old partners.

Dr. Brandes was also to be a partner of the new firm, as I had wished him to be one, although he had no capital; but considering him, as I have said already to be my best friend in the world, I wanted to have him at my side to watch closely over my own private interests, which partly would become his own also, as I told him very often. Also I saw in him the only physician able to attend to me in my sickness.

To keep him near me, I should have made any concessions. I thought I should die if he was going to leave me. Mssrs. Wetzlar had been represented to me by him to have acquired already some $10,000, which I, together with their kno[w]ledge, business experience, a.s.f., considered as large an investment, or even a larger one, than the one I was going to make. Mr. Wetzlar, Senior, then told my father, that in order to do a profitable business, it would be proper for one of the firm to go to New York to make some purchase. My father agreed to procure for him letters of credit for New York. They then proceded to San Francisco where my mother in the meantime had arrived. No house, however, wanted to give such letters of credit as they wanted, and Mr. Wetzlar, Senior, with a small amount of money, hardly enough to pay his passage, left for New York in the month of January 1850. Mr. Julius Wetzlar, who then managed the affairs here alone, told me that his brother had sufficient credit in New York to obtain goods with. He then showed me in inventory, I have now not the least doubt a false one, by which he convinced me of the existence of a good stock of goods on hand in the store at Sacramento City, as well as of a well supplied establishment under the management of Mssrs. Stratton & Venner,[59] two of their partners at Auburn. I do not recollect now at what sum he had estimated the whole of it; the house and lot on J Street,[60] the first a frame covered with a canvass room, was also estimated at a very exorbitant rate. He showed to me that by realising everything belonging to the old firm, each partner would receive for his share the amount of $4,000 or more, that he for the present, everything being invested in goods and real estate, had no ready money to pay the three other partners off with, but that they, however, would consent to receive notes payable some time later each for the amount of $4,000, signed by our new firm. Dr. Brandes told me he had full confidence in the statements of Mr. Wetzlar relating to their financial position, that he knew the real estate to be worth what it was estimated at and that he thought these notes could be given without any danger. I accepted of everything. Mr. Venner, one of the partners, remained as a clerk to us and went to settle the business at Auburn, which establishment we had resolved to bring to a close.[61] The new firm of Wetzlar, Sutter & Co., after this

---

[59] A Francis Stratton appears as a witness on several Sacramento records of land sales. Benjamin Fenner, whose name Sutter misspells, is listed as a member of the firm. (*Placer Times,* Mar. 16, 1850.)

[60] Located on J Street between Third and Fourth Streets. (*Sacramento Transcript,* June 22, 1850.)

[61] In the *Placer Times* of Mar. 16, 1850, appeared these two announcements:
DISSOLUTION OF CO-PARTNERSHIP.
The partnership heretofore existing between the undersigned in Sacramento City and Auburn, under the firm of Wetzlar & Co. is this day dissolved by mutual consent.
The business affairs of said firm will be adjusted by Julius Wetzlar, who is alone authorized to collect the debts due the same, and settle all claims and legal demands against said firm.
GUSTAVUS WETZLAR,
JULIUS WETZLAR,
BENJ. FENNER,
CORNELIUS SCHERMERHORN,
FRANCIS STRATTON.
Sacramento City, Feb. 25, 1850.

contract, was then to pay to the three leaving partners of the old firm, Wetzlar & Co., the amount of $12,000 and assumed at the same time all the liabilities of it. Already in this absurd transaction I was outrageously deceived, because I afterwards found the goods on hand to consist of a very paltry, small and, for the greatest part unsuitable, assortments for the market, and I have reasons to believe the same in regard to the Auburn establishment I never have seen. My father could not give me money, as he had agreed to do, when the time fixed came. I then, pressed by my partners, went to Hock Farm and obtained some money from my mother and some more by the sale of some horses and mules (which then yet belonged in fact to me, as I had not conferred the personal property back to my father yet), altogether about from $3,000 to $4,000, not more.

This money I delivered to Mr. Wetzlar; I am satisfied now that it was spent in paying debts of which he never had spoken to me before entering in any arrangements, for the most part moneys which had been deposited with them for safekeeping and which they had used for their own emergencies. This I saw then, but there was such a spell on me that I could not free myself from the influence of these men, and in the contrary fell only deeper in their net every day. A small amount was laid out also for improvements on the building on J Street which were absolutely necessary. My father had given as a token of his friendship to Dr. Brandes a share in the new town of Elisa,[62] an-

---

CO-PARTNERSHIP.

The undersigned have this day entered into copartnership, under the firm of Wetzlar, Sutter & Co. in Sacramento City and Auburn, North Fork.

GUSTAVUS WETZLAR,
JULIUS WETZLAR,
JOHN A. SUTTER, JR.
C. BRANDES.

Sacramento City, Feb. 25, 1850.

[62] Eliza, named after Captain Sutter's daughter, was one of the many "paper towns" that sprang up along the rivers. It was located on the east side of the Feather River just below Marysville and was founded about Jan., 1850, by Captain Sutter at the suggestion of members of the Kennebec Co. The agent of the company, Dr. McCullough, though first interested in Marysville, became alarmed for the future of that town when several river steamers grounded down the river, and bought an interest in Eliza. Lienhard became heavily involved in Eliza, and erected a building there, but persuaded Sutter, Jr., to buy him out. An *alcalde*

other share I received, and Mr. Wetzlar bought one which was duly paid for by him, there having been furnished by him several times to me provisions for Hock Farm. The doctor for the benefit of the firm also bought some property for several thousand dollars at the town of Nicholas[63] on speculation. Mr. Wetzlar, Dr. Brandes, as well as I myself, pressed on by them, remonstrated with my father, telling him that we were altogether stopped in business operations by his not having complied with his promise of procuring the said $30,000. He then transferred to me, as an equivalent to this amount, his interest in what was called the Zinc House property, which was owned by him, Brannan and others. At a division of this property the Zinc House, by chance, as well as some other property, fell to my share.[64] Although then in reality quite without value, this property was considered to be worth a great deal in the spirit of the times. I then transferred to each of my partners one-fourth interest in all the property I owned, and I received in compensation one-fourth part of interest in the real estate and goods of the firm, so that each of us owned an equal share of all the property. Here again I was made their dupe, as I must confess, I do not know how. With great difficulties a part of the $12,000 were raised to pay off the other men, the part, in fact about two thirds of this amount only, were paid on the occasion when Brannan and others paid their first installment to me.[65] We did no

was elected and a few buildings put up, but Eliza's prospects began to fade, and by June, 1850, the town had completely collapsed and its few residents moved elsewhere. (Chamberlain, *Hist. Yuba County,* p. 42; Lienhard, *Pioneer,* pp. 233–236, 259; Ramey, *Beginnings of Marysville,* p. 23.)

[63] Here, on the Sacramento River just below the mouth of the Bear, Nicolaus Altgeier settled in 1842, operated a ferry, and during the gold rush established a trading post. Early in 1850 he laid out the town of Nicolaus which by April had some twenty-four houses. It was one of the many towns which laid claim to being the head of navigation. During the feverish development of river towns it became for a time the county seat of Sutter County. (Bancroft, *Calif.,* II, 691; VI, 488; *Alta Calif.,* Aug. 7, 1850.)

[64] "The zinc house was built by Hensley, Schoolcraft and myself," said Sutter, Sr. "I occupied a room in that house, and had my library in it. After an arrangement with the other proprietors, I gave this house, with certain others, to my son." (*Placer Times,* June 28, 1850, reprinted *Sacramento Union,* Feb. 23, 1858.) Bancroft places the building on J Street between Front and Second, and says it was built in 1849. (*Calif.,* VI, 449.)

[65] This was for young Sutter's Sacramento property, about which he writes later.

business because there were no funds nor goods on hand to do it with; all was a mere show to keep up appearances. Mr. Wetzlar, Senior, wrote from New York he had been very unsuccessful and that he even had been obliged to borrow money to pay his board, a.s.f. I always was sick and very weak; I saw that we did not any business. Mr. Wetzlar told me that I had disappointed them and that my father was the only cause of their bad circumstances and precarious situation; difficulties with Mr. Lienhardt, which it would be long to mention here, broke in upon me; I finally was worked up to a dreadful state of excitement by all these circumstances. I gradually became convinced by the tales of my partners and of other men, who took pleasure in reporting to me the bad policy and follies of my father, that in a few years my father would have squandered all his property, that then all our family would be left without a dollar to subsist on, and finally that it was high time for me to interfere and to save whatever I could from the general ruin for my own and the rest of the family's benefit. By which means I was brought to this state of feverish, insane state of my mind, I am unable to say. But think of the circumstances already mentioned, the dreadful disorder of my father's affairs, of the way he then by a great many scoundrels was abused, and then of the exaggeration and disfiguration with which such reports reached me; and I hope that if I committed great faults which cannot be excused and of which I even do not try to vindicate myself, on the other side, if anybody puts himself in my true position, I shall not be condemned altogether.

I sometimes hardly knew what I did and was rather an automaton in the hands of Dr. Brandes than anything else. I then in this insane state of my mind, as it properly may be called, went with Dr. Brandes, who never lost sight of me, to Hock Farm and demanded of my father to transfer to me his entire interest in Sacramento City and a square mile of land between the city and Sutterville[66] he said he

---

[66] For one dollar Sutter sold to his son, on May 7, 1850, "all my right, title and interest in Sacramento City Upper California consisting in town lots and buildings standing thereupon." (Sacramento County, *Deed Books,* vol. C, p. 224.) For another dollar, on May 11, Sutter transferred to August *one-half* square mile of land along the Sacramento River, between Sacramento and Sutterville, and adjoining the south property already owned by young Sutter. (*Ibid.,* pp. 223–224.)

owned yet. I, after a very violent scene with my father, obtained a deed to this purpose, and gave him a document transferring his personal property back to him, as also another one relinquishing any other claims of mine against him for the future. Of a great many things which I am told passed then, I have not the slightest recollection, and, if anybody else did tell me of them, I always with a good conscience denied the facts, even to my brother, until my mother herself tells me now the same thing. I must have been out of my senses. I returned to Sacramento City with Dr. Brandes; Mr. Schoolcraft, then the agent still of my father, hardly could give us any information in regard to the property and lots sold or yet unsold. I went with Mr. Wetzlar to San Francisco where I received from Mr. Peachy a list of the lots he had not sold yet. Mr. Peachy had had to sell every alternate block and Mr. Schoolcraft the others. However, there had been committed in Sacramento City so many irregularities, so many had been sold twice or even three times that it was impossible, or at least it appeared to me impossible, to sell any lots without running the risk of falling more and more into difficulties and law suits without end. I always continued sick, and having seen a great many people go away and leave for some other country, I also became desirous of retiring to some other part of the world, I did not care where, provided I should enjoy good health and not hear any more of these confusions and my unpleasant business altogether. Dr. Brandes advised me to settle with Mr. Wetzlar first as a commencement and expressed also his intention to return to the eastern states. Some days afterwards Mr. Wetzlar proposed to me he would take in settlement of all his claims against the concern the whole Zinc House property and leave to me and to the doctor all the other property belonging to the firm; and suggested to me also that Dr. Brandes, as his share, ought to receive from me the sum of $10,000, with the remark that, although we had not done any business, our real estate had risen much in value. I told him I would reflect upon it and after a consultation with Dr. Brandes again agreed to everything. The doctor and I transferred to Mr. Wetzlar our interests in the Zinc House property, and then I gave to the doctor my note for $10,000 payable on the first of June. This was the end of our commercial speculations, after which dissolution of partnership all the liabilities of the concern fell to my lot.[67] Mr. Wetzlar and the doctor offered to attend further to my business, until it should be entirely arranged. I was anxious to settle everything in such a manner as to be able to leave with Dr. Brandes. I was afraid that if I should stay all the hot season without the doctor at Sacramento City, I should die. I almost could not wait patiently for the moment when my affairs would allow me to leave a country where, since the day of my arrival, I had been continually under mental and bodily pains. I was in debt and did not know how to get out of it. I would have to pay shortly some $6,000 yet to Mssrs. Venner and Schemerhorn,[68] former partners of Mr. Wetzlar, $10,000 to Dr. Brandes, some $2,000 due to Mr. N. Altgeier[69] or his agents for lots in Nicholas, a.s.f., some lawyer bills. The squatters had commenced to be troublesome.[70] The taxes this year were going to be enormous, as I anticipated.[71] I was afraid of selling single lots, or blocks, not knowing to a

---

[67] The firm of Wetzlar, Sutter & Co. was dissolved by mutual consent on May 28, 1850, and Sutter, Jr., was "solely charged with the liquidation of the business." (*Alta Calif.*, May 31, 1850.)

[68] Cornelius Schermerhorn was a member of the firm of Wetzlar & Co.

[69] Nicolaus Altgeier was a German trapper with the Hudson's Bay Co. who came to California in 1840 and worked for Sutter at the Fort. One '49er speaks of him as a "Tremendous Scoundril." (Kerr, "Irishman in the Gold Rush," in *Calif. Hist. Soc. Quarterly*, VIII [1929], 23.) See also note 63.

[70] Free soilers soon began to squat on Sutter's lands and on the lots already sold by him. Often they put up shacks, built fences, and down the barrels of their frontier rifles defied the owners and authorities to eject them, particularly after they discovered the flaw in Vioget's survey of New Helvetia. Conflicts occurred frequently, culminating in the bloody squatter riots of Aug., 1850. (Plumbe, *Faithful Translation of the Papers Respecting the Grant Made by Governor Alvarado to John A. Sutter;* Royce, "Squatter Riot of '50 in Sacramento," in *Overland Monthly*, VI, ser. 2 [1855], 225–246; Colville, *Sacramento Directory, 1853–54,* p. 16–17, 25–34.)

[71] On Apr. 30, 1850, the city voted $250,000 for levees alone, and this sum, combined with other civil expenses including extravagant salaries, quickly boosted the indebtedness to $400,000. (Bancroft, *Calif.*, VI, 453, 455–456.) "The flood of the winter of 1849–'50 at Sacramento City," wrote Burnett, "not only caused the prices of property and rents to decline heavily, but increased the taxation for city purposes enormously. The rate of taxation that year for State, county, and city purposes, at Sacramento City, amounted to ten per cent. of the assessed value of the property." (*Recollections,* p. 391.) Young Sutter's property was assessed $14,605.85 for city taxes, and $5,200 for county and state taxes, the second high-

certainty which were sold and which were not. I had had already to settle some difficulties arising from double sales made by my father and his many agents. I did not know what to do. I became more and more confuse[d]. I suggested one day to Mr. Wetzlar that I should like to sell my whole interest in California, if there could be found anybody to buy it. He said that it was difficult to find buyers for so large an amount of property but that he would exert himself for the purpose of finding buyers. In a few days he informed me that in fact he had found parties who should feel inclined to buy my whole interest if I should put a reasonable price on it. He insinuated to me then that Mr. Sam. Brannan and some gentlemen from San Francisco were the parties. He never said a word to me of his going to take an interest in the purchase then. I told him that I was willing to hear the proposals of these gentlemen, that I would sell cheap with the condition that they never after the sale should claim anything from me, that they should pay the taxes this year and that they should carry on on their own account all the lawsuits which might have resulted or still result from double sales, squatter difficulties, a.s.f.

He very soon informed me that Mr. Brannan and others were willing to give me the amount of $125,000 for the whole amount of real estate I had and that, taking into consideration the conditions I had stipulated to them, they would not give anything more. I found [it] to be not enough. Mr. Wetzlar and Dr. Brandes then remonstrated with me that I never would find a better opportunity to effect a sale, that it was a rare chance, that these gentlemen were going to buy all my interests, [become] involved in law suits [and] disputes about the title, even not knowing what lots and lands were really mine, that they were going to have difficulties with squatters, that they were going to pay a great deal of taxes on real estate which did not produce any rents whatever, that they were going to pay to me the sum of $125,000 with the condition of never having any right whatever to claim anything from me, and that with this sum, even after paying my liabilities which I have mentioned before, under no responsibilities

---

est single assessment at that time in Sacramento. (Culver, *Sacramento City Directory, 1851*, p. 83.)

whatever to these parties, I should be enabled to live anywhere in the world as an independent man. They also alluded to my bad state of health, expressing their opinion that I never would recover my health here and that it was high time for me to change climate, as the only remedy left to me. He told me further that these gentlemen, to enable me at once to pay off my debts, would be willing to pay $25,000 on my delivering to them the conveyance, [an]other $25,000 as a second installment on the last of October [1850] and the balance of $75,000 in one year from the date of the deed. I finally agreed to this proposal and Mr. Wetzlar went to communicate it to the parties. I in all this time had seen Mr. Brannan only once when he had come to see me with Mr. Wetzlar, I then being confined to my bed. I do not recollect any particulars of this visit, where however nothing important was spoken about. Mr. Wetzlar offered to me to attend to the drawing up of the document, a.s.f., and on an evening by candlelight, I do not recollect the date of the ominous day,[72] he having told me that everything was ready, I in his and the doctor's company went to the office of Mssrs. Marshal & Stanley[73] where Mssrs. Brannan, Bruce[74] and, I think also Graham,[75] already were waiting.

I never had seen the two latter gentlemen before, and *then only* Mr. Wetzlar told me that he was going to take one-fourth part of interest in the purchase himself, Mr. Brannan one-fourth part and that Mssrs. James Graham of San Francisco and Bruce of Sacramento City were the two other parties. He told me that all four were going to be responsable jointly for the fulfillment of the contract, and

---

[72] June 20, 1850. (Sacramento County, *Deed Books,* vol. D, pp. 192–193.)

[73] This firm announced the opening of their law office and real estate agency in the *Placer Times* of Dec. 15, 1849.

[74] Samuel C. Bruce, a native of Massachusetts, arrived in California during the gold rush. He is listed among a group of leading businessmen of the winter of 1849–50, and he is identified as a "real estate holder" at 110 Third Street in 1853. He was one of the original members of the San Francisco Stock Exchange, organized in 1861. (Colville, *Sacramento Directory, 1853–54;* Bancroft, *Calif.,* VII, 668.)

[75] A James A. Grahame, a Hudson's Bay Co. employee, was at Fort Vancouver in 1845, and again in 1848–49. He had probably arrived at San Francisco by 1849. (C. J. Pike, "Petitions of Oregon Settlers, 1838–1848," *Oregon Hist. Quarterly,* XXXIV [1933], 230; Historical Records Survey, *Calendar Major Jacob Rink Snyder Collection,* p. 40.)

I therefore knowing Mr. Brannan, although I never had been acquainted with Mssrs. Bruce and Graham, had full confidence in them. As a matter of form the document was read to me. On my asking Mr. Wetzlar why they only were called in the document my agents, he said that it was a mere matter of form, that he had examined the document and that all was in order. I then signed it and Mr. Marshal being also a notary public, the ackno[w]ledgement was taken immediately.

I have been told since that Mr. Marshal for his trouble of drawing up so able a document received from these gentlemen the amount of $2,000 as his fees. I never had read the deed, or whatever it is, myself. I had such an unbounded confidence in Dr. Brandes and Wetzlar that I without the least suspicion of their treacherous conduct fell a victim to their scheme. Through my sickness my head had grown so weak, my memory and the capacities of my mind so debilitated that I was not able to judge of any important matter, less so of a document drawn up with so much subtility in a language which was not my own either. I now really do not comprehend how I could do what I then did. I further constituted Mr. Julius Wetzlar my private attorney to sell some furniture, a.s.f., which I still had, to collect some bills, some notes which I held, as also to receive the payments of Mssrs. Brannan, Bruce and Graham and consequently of himself, in the case I should not be in the country at the time of an installment falling due, another act which I cannot account for; I repeat, I do not understand how I could commit such acts whose absurdity I afterwards, although too late, with terror discovered. I am convinced that anybody, even a child quite unacquainted with business, would not have committed such acts in a sound state of his mind. After having gone once more to Hock Farm to take [leave] of my mother, my brothers and sister, I in company of Dr. Brandes and Mr. Wetzlar went to San Francisco in order to be ready to set out by the steamer on the first of July. Mr. Wetzlar just then had received letters from his brother, Mr. Gustavus Wetzlar, from New York, informing him that he had managed to obtain some goods on credit and that for the amount of these goods he had drawn bills on him. Two of the bills, I think amounting

about to $6,000, had already arrived and had been presented to Mr.
Wetzlar, who requested me then, after having already consented to
receive the part of the sum of $25,000 (of which he should have been
one-fourth part) at a later date, to let him have yet all the money I
could spare for this emergency, he not having any means on hand to
honor the bills. He promised to me to pay to me his part of the first
installment and to refund to me the money I should lend to him as
soon as the said goods should have arrived, and that he would send it
to me, wherever I should be, as well as other moneys which he would
be able to collect by and by. I gave him the gold I thought I could
spare, and when I left here on the steamer I had not large amounts
of money at my command as general rumors used to represent. I only
had the quite moderate sum of $1,400 in gold dust in my possession
then, all I had left of the first $18,000 after having paid my liabilities
to the former partners of Mr. Wetzlar, to Dr. Brandes, to some lawyers, to the agents of N. Altgeier for lots in Nicholas and after having
lent some $2,000 I think, to Mr. Wetzlar.

In San Francisco I learnt that Mr. Bruce had sold one-half of his
interest to Mr. W. M. Howard[76] and that Mr. Graham had disposed
of one-half of his share to Mr. Thomas Warbass.[77] I then left with Dr.
Brandes, not having one single document, not one single note, nor
any other instrument for the protection of my interests in my hands,
in blind and unbounded confidence in Wetzlar, and I once more declare it with only the small sum of about $1,400 in gold dust after

---

[76] A native of Boston, W. D. M. Howard first came to California in 1839, was
a trader and eventually became one of the country's leading merchants. He placed
Sam Brannan in charge of his company's branch in Sacramento after the gold
discovery, and then financed Brannan when the Mormon leader opened a store
at Mormon Diggings. Howard died in 1856 at the age of thirty-seven. Among all
early San Francisco traders he was one of the finest, most scrupulous, and popular.
(Bancroft, *Calif.*, III, 788–789; D. S. Watson, "Great Extra of the California
Star of Apr. 1, 1848," *Calif. Hist. Soc. Quarterly*, XI [1932], 135–136.)

[77] Thomas A. Warbass arrived in California in 1840 or 1842. In 1850 he was
the senior member of the banking and real estate firm of Warbass & Co., which
included William S. Heyle and Dr. John F. Morse. The purchase from Grahame
cost $25,625. In the late summer of 1850 a financial crisis in Sacramento caused
several of the city's banking houses, including Warbass & Co., to close their doors.
(Bancroft, *Calif.*, V, 766; Davis, *Illus. Hist. Sacramento County*, p. 140; Colville,
Sacramento Directory, 1853–54, p. 25; Sacramento County, *Deed Books*, vol. D,
pp. 279–282.)

having paid my passage. I had not fixed on any place to go to; my only object had been to leave California;[78] I had letters of introduction to Lima, Guayaquil, a.s.f. It would have been immaterial to me to make a voyage to China, or to go to Europe or to the eastern states. At Acapulco I went on shore. The spell of Dr. Brandes I was in was broken by another important incident of my life,[79] and I was so delighted with the place that I at once concluded to stop there at least for some time.

Dr. Brandes proceeded on the steamer to Panama; I never since have heard of him although I several times wrote to him in regard to two very valuable saddles of mine which were so engaged in the baggage on board the steamer that they could not be taken out and of which he had promosed to me to take care. In the last letter, I wrote to him from San Francisco after my return from Acapulco, after many other unsuccessful ones by which I had requested him to send me those saddles, I called him even a thief. He never answered to me and has sent the saddles since without a word to me at Hock Farm, used and in a very bad order. At Acapulco I made the acquaintance of Mr. Julius Lecacheux, a French gentleman who with the ship "Espadon" had come from San Francisco to this latter port with some goods.[80] I gradually recovered my health at Acapulco to a certain extent and finding that the climate did agree so well with me, I concluded to stay there, and as the commerce of the place then promised to become very important and was improving fast, Acapulco having become a station of the P. M. S. S. Company, I thought of going into some kind of business. Also I was induced to stay at Acapulco by its continual, regular connections with California and its little distance from the place where my interest[s] still were.

---

[78] They left for Panama on the steamer *California*, July 1, 1850. (*Alta Calif.*, July 1, 2, 1850.)

[79] This was his meeting with Señorita María del Carmen Rivas, whom he married before the year was out. (Hull to the writer, Feb. 21, 1941.)

[80] Julius Le Cacheux and L. Galley are listed in Parker, *San Francisco Directory, 1852–53*, as wine merchants at 54 Merchant Street and as wine importers at 64 Front Street. The French ship *Espadon*, Captain Charenton, cleared San Francisco for Acapulco June 6, and probably arrived late that same month. (*Alta Calif.*, June 7, 1850.)

Mr. Lecacheux offered to me to become my partner and as a commencement of our business to put on shore at once his goods. We agreed that I with another gentleman who had come with him, Mr. Lafforgue, as a clerk, should stay at Acapulco and that Mr. Lecacheux should forthwith proceed to San Francisco to receive from Mr. Wetzlar all the funds he might have in his hands for my account, as also to receive the $25,000 which would fall due on the last of October. This was in the month of September 1850. I never have had to regret until today of having made the acquaintance of these gentlemen, although I proved to them rather a loss than a gain, my misfortunes influencing also greatly their own business; I always found them to be loyal and true friends and am sure that even now their feelings towards me have not undergone any change. Mr. Lecacheux left with the necessary power of attorney[81] from me for San Francisco.

A few days after Mr. Lecacheux's departure, Mr. Bruce passed at Acapulco on his way to the eastern states; he came to see me and told me that I had better keep a sharp eye on Mr. Wetzlar, that he was a swindler, a designing rogue and that he had obtained from him, Bruce, several times under various pretences money which he had not been able to recover from him again notwithstanding his great efforts. At the same time the news of the failure of the firm Simmons, Hutchinson & Co.[82] and some other land speculators came to my ears. Mr. Bruce also told me there had arrived in California a general crisis and that real estate had fallen greatly in value. These news startled me a good deal; I commenced to conceive some fears and suspicion in regard to Mr. Wetzlar and was very anxious to receive news from Mr. Lecacheux.

This gentleman, soon after his arrival at San Francisco at the end

---

[81] He obtained the power of attorney on Jan. 24, 1851. (Sacramento County, *Powers of Attorney*, vol. A, pp. 333–336.)

[82] Simmons, Hutchinson & Co. ran the steamers *McKim* and *Gold Hunter* on the Sacramento River in 1849 and 1850, were commission merchants at the Clay Street Wharf, San Francisco, and also dealt in Sacramento real estate. The senior member of the firm was Bezer Simmons, a shipmaster who had been on the coast for some years. He died in 1850, and the firm failed. (Bancroft, *Calif.*, V, 720; *Alta Calif.*, May 23, 1850; *Placer Times*, Nov. 3, 1849; Kimball, *San Francisco City Directory, 1850;* Davis, *Illus. Hist. Sacramento County*, p. 140.)

of October,[83] had presented himself to Mr. Wetzlar who, it appears, treated him as if he had no confidence in him and always gave him evasive answers and confuse[d] replys to his direct question whether he had any moneys belonging to me in his hands. After the calculation I had made, Mr. Wetzlar owed me then, separately from his liabilities to me jointly with Brannan and others, about $12,000, moneys which he had realised out of personal property I had left, bills he had collected, his part of the first installment to be paid yet and gold I had lent to him. During my stay at Acapulco I only had received from him some things I had requested him to send to me and which I on the occasion of my marriage wanted to present to my wife. For these he made me an exorbitant bill of some $800, and the disinterested friend who owed me no favors at all charged me even some $80 traveling expenses from Sacramento City to San Francisco for the voyage he had been obliged to make for the purpose of purchasing and forwarding to me the said things. Mr. Lecacheux, not knowing what to think of Wetzlar, went to consult with Mr. Dillon,[84] the French consul, who gave him the advice to employ in my interest some eminent lawyers and recommended to him as such Mssrs. Burrit, Yale & Musson.[85] Mr. Lecacheux then explained his business to these gentlemen, who informed him that my presence here was necessary. Consequently he wrote to me to Acapulco to leave all the busi-

---

[83] He arrived on the *Columbus*, Oct. 12, 1850. (*Alta Calif.*, Oct. 13, 1850.)

[84] Irish by descent and French by citizenship, Patrick or Patrice Dillon had collaborated with Guizot on several of his histories. He was sent to San Francisco as French consul and became quite unpopular in California because he stood on his diplomatic dignity and refused to testify in an important court case. He was later promoted to consul-general in Santo Domingo and died in Paris on Oct. 18, 1857. (*Alta Calif.*, July 2, 1854; San Francisco *Bulletin*, Dec. 2, 1857; Ernest de Massey, "Frenchman in the Gold Rush," *Calif. Hist. Soc. Quarterly*, V [1926], 344.)

[85] Samuel L. Burritt, Gregory Yale, and Eugene Musson. Of the three, Yale became the most prominent. A southerner from Richmond, he came to San Francisco in 1849, where he opened the legal office of Yale & Nunes in the adobe building on the Plaza. He began to specialize in mining law, water rights, and Mexican land titles, and in 1867 published *Mining Claims and Water Rights in California*. He died in 1871. (Parker, *San Francisco Directory, 1852–53;* Morgan, *San Francisco City Directory, 1852;* Kimball, *San Francisco City Directory, 1850; San Francisco Chronicle,* June 18, 1871; Pioneer file, California State Library.)

ness in the hands of Mr. Lafforgue and to come as soon as possible to San Francisco, my business requiring my presence immediately, and that he with Mssrs. Burrit, Yale & Musson should take until my arrival all the preliminary steps in my affairs which could be done. I left Acapulco on the 24th of December 1850 and arrived here on the 8th of January 1851. Mr. Lecacheux, the very day of my arrival, introduced me to Mssrs. Burrit, Yale & Musson, who already had obtained a copy of the contract with Brannan and others and had pronounced it to be a masterpiece, of which they after a careful examination said that it could not be attacked in any way whatever, that I had been dreadfully imposed upon and that I was left altogether at the mercy of Mssrs. Brannan and others. I entered into an agreement with them that instead of paying any fees to them they were to receive one-fourth part of all the moneys they should be able to collect for me; they agreed on their side to go to work forthwith and to do their utmost in the affair. It was further agreed that the same day I should proceed to Sacramento in company with Mr. Gregory Yale to demand from Mr. Wetzlar a full statement of his administration of my affairs and a final settlement. His power of attorney the same day was revoked.

Immediately after our arrival at Sacramento I went to see Mr. Wetzlar, who, when I met with him, was already informed that I had arrived in company of a lawyer. Somebody had seen and recognised us, and reported to him the news, I imagine. The rest he, of course, easily suspected. I soon requested him to give to me, as a customary and reasonable thing, a statement of my affairs, an account in writing of moneys he had received or paid out for me.

Then he answered to me sneeringly, w[h]ether I took him to be a fool, to give me such a document which would expose him entirely? He stated further that he knew very well that Mr. Yale had come with me, that he knew the object of our visit, and that he in no way would consent to do anything proposed by Mr. Yale, and finally that if I would make any noise in this business I should obtain nothing from him, having no proofs whatever in my hands against him, but that if I would keep still and wait a few days, he would settle the business amicably with me to my entire satisfaction, that he had no money on hand, but that he would give me in settlements goods which he had received from New York and which at that moment were in the Zinc House.

I saw that I was obliged to submit and to make "bonne mine au mauvais jeu," being entirely entrapped in Wetzlar's clutches. I informed Mr. Yale of the result of my interview with Wetzlar. He agreed with me that it would be best for me to try to come to an amicable settlement with Wetzlar, recommended to me the greatest care and caution and returned again to San Francisco.

The day after, Wetzlar showed to me an account he had made out. In this account, which he took great care not to let out of his hands, he had made me charge of the bill of some $800 of things sent to me in Acapulco, his bill of traveling expenses already mentioned and some other unjust and extravagant charges I do not recollect; but what in my eyes is and always will be the "Ne plus ultra," the highest perfection, of impudence and rascality, is a charge of $1,000 he made as commission for his trouble he had taken to find parties willing to buy my real estate, where he had taken an interest himself! Commision for a sale, and such a sale! Made to himself and others!

I think this only instance would be enough to show Mr. Wetzlar's character in a true light.

He returned to me then two notes of one thousand dollars each given to me by Dr. Perry[86] some time ago for real estate, and in full settlement of everything gave me goods consisting of segars, wine and molasses, a.s.f., I think to the amount of some $6,000. These goods had been estimated by Mr. D. K. Brannan[87] and another gentleman whose name I do not recollect and at whose estimation I had agreed with Wetzlar to take the goods. These goods I took down to San Francisco, and Mssrs. Lecacheux & Galley sold them not without a new considerable loss to me, as they have been estimated in Sacramento to[o] highly for the San Francisco market, or even for any

[86] Perhaps Dr. Alexander Perry, who came out in 1847 as surgeon of the New York Volunteers. (Bancroft, *Calif.*, IV, 774.)

[87] D. K. Brannan was listed as the agent of Brannan & Co., located at 43 Front Street, Sacramento, in the Sacramento city directory of 1851.

market. Dr. Perry afterwards paid me one thousand dollars in cash which I gradually spent for my expenses in San Francisco and in purchasing some things I sent to my wife to Acapulco, and for the remaining thousand dollars he returned to me one block of eight lots in Sacramento City, for which property I requested to execute a deed to Mr. Julius Lecacheux to whom I wanted to insure as much as possible my debt resulting from goods put on shore at Acapulco, as well as from expenses he kindly had incurred for me in my affairs.

Mssrs. Burrit, Yale & Musson informed me that they had had an interview with Mr. Brannan and, I think, also with Mr. Howard, from whom they had learnt that they had never come in possession of the square mile of land between Sacramento City and Sutterville[88] mentioned in the conveyance and which they said had been conveyed already before he [Sutter, Sr.] deeded it to me, to Dr. White[89] and others; that for this reason they wanted to deduct $40,000 from the total amount of the sale, that also further they would deduct another amount of $20,000 from the original sum, which they stated to be the amount of taxes paid by them on the from me acquired property. I told these gentlemen that I always had been in the belief that I was under no responsability whatever to Mssrs. Brannan and others after

---

[88] The square mile spoken of here was really only one-half of that area. It was described as a "certain tract of land situate on the Sacramento river commencing at a point on the East bank of said River adjoining the land owned by George McKinstry, running thence up the said River bank along the low water line One half mile, thence on a direct line back from said river One mile, thence on a line parallel to the aforesaid River line Southerly, One half mile and thence to the place of beginning. Being that certain tract of land situate, lying and being between the Southerly boundary of Sacramento City, and the town called 'Sutter' or 'Sutterville.' " (Sacramento County, *Deed Books,* vol. D, pp. 192–193.)

[89] Dr. Thomas J. White, who came overland in 1849, was active in medical and political circles in early Sacramento, being speaker of the assembly in 1850. He was also involved in land speculation. On May 6, 1850, five days before Captain Sutter transferred the land to his son, he sold to Dr. White and Cadwalader Ringgold, for $5,000 and an agreement to make further surveys, plans and improvements, a two-thirds interest in the waterfront from Sacramento to Sutterville. (Sacramento County, *Deed Books,* vol. D, p. 134.) This included the land lying between Front Street and the river, and obviously the elder Sutter had no right to dispose of it, since his son's deed to the city of Jan. 2, 1849, had reserved it to owners of lots on Front Street. (Sacramento County, *Deed Books,* vol. A, p. 164.) August, mentally and physically upset at the time, either declined to contest it or was unaware of his father's sale.

the contract I had made with them. They said they would investigate the matter further and requested me to call from time to time at their office for further information.

I did so every two or three days for nearly three months, never learning anything new. These gentlemen assumed some kind of a patronising air towards me which would have vexed not only me, I am sure. I recollect one instance when I was waiting for one of these gentlemen, Mr. Gregory Yale, in their office. Opening the door and seeing me he said without further ceremony: *Mr. Sutter, your affair is still in a "statu quo,"* and passed by majestically without paying any more attention to his poor unhappy client.

Probably Mr. Yale had thought to overawe me by his profound learning and kno[w]ledge of latin.

Mr. Lecacheux and I then formed the opinion that these gentlemen were either afraid to proceed against men like Mssrs. Brannan and Howard, with whom we heard they were in business connection or rather that they sided with them, instead of defending my interests. Mr. Brannan then, I think it was in March [1851], came and made me direct propositions to settle the difficulties, offering for him and in the name of the other parties to pay to me $40,000 as the reduced price of my property on the first of July next.

Mr. Brannan had hit the right moment. I was so exasperated by the conduct of Mssrs. Burrit, Yale & Musson just then that he found but very little difficulty in persuading me that it was the best thing I could do. Also I was without any money and indebted to Mssrs. Lecacheux and Galley, who generously had come to my aid and furnished me with the necessary means to live with. I also was anxious to return to Acapulco where I had left my wife and where I thought I should, under the then very favorable circumstances, soon be able to recover from such a severe loss. I told then Mr. Brannan that I wanted some money immediately to pay my most necessary expenses.

He then remarked that he had but very little money at this moment but that, however, he would try to let me have some. I then, I may say, forced by want and necessity, agreed to his proposition. He immediately communicated my resolution to the other parties, and a

few days after this I signed a new conveyance to them, receiving from
them the following values:

from Mr. Saml. Brannan his note for	$4,750.
from Mr. W. M. Howard his do ”	”4,750.
from Mr. Bruce his do ”	”4,750.
from Mr. T. Shillaber[90] his do ”	”4,750.
from Mr. Wetzlar his do ”	”9,500.
from Mr. James Graham his do ”	”9,500.
all payable the first of July 1851	$38,000.

also from Mssrs. Brannan, Howard and Shillaber
$250 each   750.

from Mssrs. Graham, and Wetzlar who were to pay
also $500 each and from Mr. Bruce who was to pay
$250 for his share, I had received   1,250.

their notes payable on demand $40,000.

Mr. Theodore Shillaber had bought from Mr. Brannan one-half
of his interest in the purchase. On the other side, Mr. T. Warbass
having failed, Mr. Graham had been obliged to take back the part
which he had disposed of to this gentleman. But I even had not time
to collect these notes payable on demand, before Mssrs. Burrit, Yale
& Musson, through one of the parties themselves, had received information of this transaction and obtained an order from the Superior
Court forbidding the parties to make any payments whatever to me,
stating that they were interested in my affairs for $12,000. They also
swore before the court, that I was on the point of absconding and
leaving secretly the country, when they knew well that I had no idea
of leaving before collecting the said bills; and the sheriff left me the

---

[90] Theodore Shillaber, after trading between California and Mexico in the late
1840's, apparently settled in San Francisco about 1849. In 1850 he was a member
of the firm of Everett & Co., agent for the early steamers *Fire Fly, Chesapeake,
Tehama,* and others. ("Journal of Captain John Paty," *Calif. Hist. Soc. Quarterly,* XIV [1935], 329, 333, 336, 337; Kimball, *San Francisco City Directory,
1850.*) On Feb. 28, 1851, Brannan certified that he held his one-fourth interest in
the property purchased from Sutter, Jr., in trust for the equal benefit of himself
and Shillaber. (Sacramento County, *Deed Books,* vol. G, p. 23.) On Sept. 18,
1855, Shillaber sold part of this property to Gilbert A. Grant for $6,250 (*ibid.,*
vol. Q, p. 96), and on Apr. 23, 1859, Shillaber and Grant released Brannan of
his trust. (*Ibid.,* vol. Z, p. 52.)

choice to go to prison or to give bail for the sum of $20,000. Mr. Lecacheux and another friend of his gave bail for me. The notes I, already before anything has been done by Mssrs. Burrit, Yale & Musson, had endorsed all to Mssrs. J. Lecacheux and S. Galley. This happened at the end of the month of March 1851.

I then fairly was involved with Mssrs. Burrit, Yale & Musson in a new lawsuit, they claiming $12,000 as their fees for what they had done in my affairs, that is to say, for hardly anything at all if it is not for having detained me three months nearly waiting in San Francisco and for having shown to me so much politeness and friendship.

They would not come to any reasonable terms, when Mr. Lecacheux had gone to see them in the matter. I then called with Mr. Lecacheux on Col. Weller.[91] I made him acquainted with the state of my affairs. Col. Weller agreed to defend me against Mssrs. Burrit, Yale and Musson, the following provisions for his fees having been made: In the case Mssrs. Burrit, Yale and Musson should obtain judgment against me for more than one thousand dollars, Col. Weller was to receive as his fees from me one thousand dollars; if, however, the judgment should be only this amount or less, he was to have $2,000. The first time the case came on, the jury gave a verdict against me for the amount of one thousand dollars in favor of Mssrs. Burrit, Yale & Musson. They appealed, however, demanding a second trial, on which another jury gave judgment against me for $5,000 in favor of my adversaries. This decision was given near the end of June. I was obliged to let have Mssrs. Burrit, Yale and Musson Mr. Howard's note, and the rest of $250 was paid to them by Mr. Brannan, who also paid to me the remaining $4,500, one thousand of which I paid to Col. Weller as his fees. So that $3,500 was all the money I received on the first of July. I delivered this sum, considering it my duty, to Mssrs. Lecacheux and Galley; they had always paid my expenses for me and I was owing to them money resulting therefrom.

---

[91] Colonel John B. Weller, an Ohio lawyer and politician who rose to military rank in the Mexican War, served as chairman of the United States-Mexican Boundary Commission in 1849 and 1850, after which he came to San Francisco and opened a law office. He later became a senator from California and in 1858 and 1859 was governor of the state. (*Dictionary of American Biography*, XIX, 628.)

Already some time ago, I had been informed by Mr. Julius Wetzlar that my father was going to sue me for moneys, *abstracted* by me, as he expressed himself, fraudulently from Hock Farm, that my father had called upon him to be a witness in the case, that he could not refuse to do so and that he, Mr. Wetzlar, advised me to pay to my father what he asked for, stating at the same time that I could pay my father with his, Mr. Wetzlar's, notes, which my father was willing to accept. He finished his letter with the irony that he would try to re-establish good understanding by and by between my father and me. Although I could have defended myself, to avoid public scandal I sent Mr. Wetzlar's two notes, one on demand for $500 and the other of $9,500 payable on the first of July 1851, to my father, informing him that from the latter note there were to be deducted the sum of one thousand dollars, for which amount I had drawn a bill on Mr. Wetzlar, in favor of Mr. Tarr,[92] a lawyer in Saco. City, to Judge Burnett who had come to see me for this purpose. (Mr. Tarr also ought to have been paid by Mssrs. Brannan, Wetzlar and others, all such costs for services of lawyers having been held forth by me as a condition of the original verbal contract.)

I am now satisfied again that this was a new contrivance of Wetzlar to get rid of his debts. I heard afterwards in the French hotel at Sacramento City that my father and Wetzlar had appeared to be on the best terms of friendship and that he had paid off my father with good words, liquor, but very little money and a few lots without much value.

I had also left for me only the notes of Bruce, Shillaber and Graham. Mssrs. Lecacheux and Galley had the note of Shillaber protested by Mr. Lucien Herrman,[93] notary public, the day it fell due,

---

[92] B. F. Tarr was a member of the Sacramento legal firm of Tarr & Cone. (Culver, *Sacramento City Directory, 1851*.) The elder Sutter once complained to Bidwell: "He made charges without conscience; I am used to be charged high fees to lawyers, but he beat all of them." (Sutter to Bidwell, Oct. 15, 1851, in Bidwell Collection.)

[93] Lucien Hermann was an attorney in San Francisco. In 1854 he was a candidate for mayor of the city but ran last in the election. (Parker, *San Francisco Directory, 1852–53*; Peyton Hurt, "Rise and Fall of the 'Know Nothings' in Calif.," in *Calif. Hist. Soc. Quarterly*, IX [1930], 27–32.) Years later he was

Mr. Shillaber having gone to China and all his property being in the hands of Mr. Argenti,[94] who told Mr. Lecacheux he could not pay anything for Mr. Shillaber's account, although he was attorney, for the reason of all his real estate being mortgaged to himself. I with Mr. Galley went up to Sacramento City, where Mr. Bruce simply declared that he was not able to pay. Mssrs. Thom and Ward[95] presented to him the notes; he told them the same thing and his note was protested by Mr. Thom, a notary public, as well as the two of Mr. Graham for $10,000, of whose whereabouts even we had no notice. Both these gentlemen, as well as Shillaber, had had the precaution, in order not to pay, to have their property transferred to other men, friends of theirs; and I, who had not taken any mortgage on their property, to facilitate to them the sales, taking Mr. Brannan's word, who told me (when I at the time of the drawing up of the last conveyance spoke to him about their giving to me a mortgage) that it would injure them only and detain them from selling lots and that therefore with a mortgage on the property they should not be able to pay me when the notes would fall due; I, believing I had to do with gentlemen and not with unprincipled swindlers, was now left without any recourse, without the least thing to fall back upon, depending only upon the generosity and the good hearts of some friends to whom I was already indebted and who, with a great disinterestedness, with no hopes ever to be paid, not abandoned me and made their best efforts, although unsuccessfully, to save what they could, paying all

---

interested in Nevada mining, serving as secretary of the Florida Silver Mining Co. of Storey County. (*Alta Calif.*, Sept. 30, 1875.)

[94] Felix or Felice Argenti was sent by Brown Bros., Colón bankers, to California in 1849 as their agent, and here he amassed a fortune of several millions, most of which he lost later in land suits against the city of San Francisco. He was for a time one of the city's most prominent bankers, but his firm failed in 1856, and though reorganized, again failed in 1857. (Bancroft, *Calif.*, VI, 335; Cross, *Financing an Empire*, I, 63, 210, 295.) Before he left California, Shillaber gave Argenti his power of attorney. (Sacramento County, *Powers of Attorney*, vol. A, pp. 471-475.)

[95] C. E. Thom, a lawyer, was listed in the Sacramento directory in 1851, and an A. F. Ward was a member of the firm of Ward & Blair, in the same year. (Culver, *Sacramento City Directory, 1851.*) An A. T. Ward, from Kentucky, was an attorney and counsellor at law a few years later. (Colville, *Sacramento Directory, 1853–54.*)

the therefrom resulting costs with their own means, and in this manner injuring their commercial operations not a little. These friends,
Mssrs. Lecacheux and Galley, requested Mssrs. Thom and Ward
to see whether they could do anything in the matter, to search the
records, a.s.f.

All the property of Bruce stood and stands now, I think, in the
name of Mr. W. M. Howard, all the property of Graham was in the
hands of Col. Weller, his assignee. Nothing could be done. Some time
later Mr. Graham offered to Mr. Lecacheux that his assignees, to
settle everything, would let him have some property in Saco. City, I
forget how many lots, and an interest in a lot on California Street in
this city. Mr. Lecacheux, who for the best of my interests saw he could
obtain nothing more, consented to this proposition, and Col. Weller,
as assignee of James Graham, conveyed to him a certain number of
lots in Sacramento City and an interest in a lot on California Street
in San Francisco as payment for the two notes amounting to $10,000,
which then were returned to Mr. Graham.

This property instead of producing anything only caused new dis-
bursements to Mssrs. Lecacheux and Galley for taxes, and although
on various occasions the property had been offered for sale privately
and at auction, it had not been possible to realise from it something.
Mssrs. Robinson and Morrison,[96] attorneys at law in Sacramento City
(Mssrs. Thom and Ward having left) were then employed by my
friends, but still without no avail. In San Francisco Mr. Mudd Clay[97]
had the affair against Shillaber in his hands. Mr. Clay, after having
received one hundred dollars from my friends as a retainer, and after
having done nothing in the case, returned to the eastern states, leav-

---

[96] Tod Robinson, born in North Carolina, arrived in Sacramento from Texas
late in 1850 and set up his law office and was joined shortly by Murray Morrison.
Few men have been defeated for office more often than Robinson: thrice for the
Supreme Court, once for attorney general, and once for clerk of the Supreme
Court in Nevada. (Shuck, *Representative and Leading Men,* pp. 495–497.) Morrison, born in Illinois, crossed the plains in 1849, and later became prominent as
a district judge in Los Angeles. (*Calif. Hist. Soc. Quarterly,* XIII [1934], 80.)

[97] Sutter, Jr., here confused the name, which was J. H. Clay Mudd. He was
a lawyer in San Francisco and was active in Whig politics. (Parker, *San Francisco
Directory, 1852–53;* Bancroft, *Calif.,* VI, 670.)

ing his business to a Mr. Wright,[98] who, I think, is still in town; to this gentleman a new retainer was to be paid. All and every payment of this kind were made by Mssrs. Lecacheux and Galley. Mr. Bruce and Mr. Shillaber came several times to see them, making them offers of settlement, declaring every time they should agree to pay something like 20% on the amount, or making some other shameful proposition. Mssrs. Lecacheux and Galley, to whose decision I had left everything, refused always indignantly to accept any so incredible offers, although it would have been in their interest to do so.

In this situation my affairs were in June 1852, as will be seen out of a letter, affixed to these statements,[99] of Mssrs. Lecacheux and Galley to me, as also out of an acct. I [had] given to me by them at the time of my leaving. It will be seen therefrom that I owed to them then the amount of $3,838, and that they held in their hands the two notes of Shillaber and Bruce and the lots taken back from Graham in Saco. City as a security for this amount, that they could dispose of these values, belonging in fact to them, after their own pleasure and best judgment. I have not heard from these gentlemen since; it would have been impossible for them to write to me; they did not know where I had gone to, because I was so disgusted with all the world, that I in my despair had concluded to hide from everybody in a corner where not even my friends would have suspected to find me.

This is the end of the drama, and I may say, with justice, the end of the second great period of my life in California, where I found myself, through the connivance and miserable tricks of some designing men, who probably now laughed at me in easy circumstances, always misunderstood by my father, even by my mother and my own brothers, with my reputation tarnished, represented everywhere as a man of loose, prodigal and intemperate habits who had squandered away his fortune, deserving nobody's help or support, with my body ruined by sickness and medicines, with a wife and child depending upon me and with poverty and misery staring to me in the face. Although my friends would not have refused a further asylum to me and

[98] Perhaps Thomas Wright, a San Francisco attorney. (Parker, *San Francisco Directory, 1852–53.*)

[99] This letter is unfortunately missing.

to my family, yet, though poor, I was too proud to abuse of their good heart any longer and preferred to hide my misery, without hardly any means, in the interior of Sonora amongst the Indians. What I with my family have suffered in Sonora I even do not try to bring to paper. If I did so, nobody ever would believe it to be the truth. It is best to pass these two long years and a half of incredible sufferings and mental agonies, in which my wife ever stood faithfully and cheeringly at my side, with silence.

I only will state that I received there a letter from my brother Alphonse[100] by which he entreated me to send to him a power of attorney, informing me that several lawyers had expressed to him their opinion that yet something could be done for me, that it was a general rumor in Sacramento City that I had been *drugged* and *poisoned* by Dr. Brandes and by Wetzlar in order to be used better as their tool in their villainous schemes. It appeared to me then that a light, a star had suddenly cleared up to me a night of darkness, the veil before my eyes fell and I gradually came to the conclusion that it must have been so. The doctor himself very often had used to tell me that he gave me very dangerous medicines, containing sometimes even poisonous substances.

I have come back to California to save, if possible, if not all at least a part of my property, in order to have my conscience free and without the reproach upon it to have neglected and abandoned everything, without having made one last effort to recover something from my general ruin for the benefit of my faithful wife and for my innocent child.

I also have come back with the intention to clear up by these writings, as well as by my future conduct in the eyes of my friends, the friends of our family and in the opinion of the public in general, the clouds thrown upon my character, a sacred duty I owe to myself, to

---

100 William Alphonse, youngest of the Sutter brothers, was now twenty-two. He left California shortly afterward as a captain with Walker's filibusters for Nicaragua. His death in 1863 at Nevada City resulted from a tropical disease contracted on that expedition. (Zollinger, *Sutter*, p. 321; Zollinger, "John Augustus Sutter's European Background," *Calif. Hist. Soc. Quarterly*, XIV [1935], 46; Greene, *Filibuster*, p. 122.)

my family and to everybody else; to defeat this way my enemies and to watch as much as possible over the interest of my poor mother, who stands on the brink of a profound abyss blindfolded and without even dreaming of it.

I finally declare solemnly that these statements are the naked truth and nothing but the truth to the best of my kno[w]ledge, as far as my memory has retained the circumstances, that I am ready to take a solemn oath upon them and that I have brought them to paper after due reflection and in an entirely quiet state of mind. San Francisco this twenty-seventh day of February in the year of Our Lord 1855.

JOHN A. SUTTER, JR.

Appendixes

Appendix I

THE CHILDREN OF JOHN A. SUTTER, JR.

THREE children were born to Sutter and his first wife, María del Carmen Rivas.

John III was born in Guaymas in 1852.[1] In 1855 he was left at Hock Farm to be raised by his grandparents. He attended John Beck's School for Boys, a Moravian school in Lititz, Pennsylvania. He married Fannie Salt of New York and in 1880 was reported to be in the tobacco business in Brooklyn.[2]

The two daughters, Anna Eliza and María del Carmen, also went east with the elder Sutters and in 1867 were placed in Linden Hall, a girls' school at Lititz. At that time Anna Eliza was eleven years old and María ten. They were living with their grandparents as late as 1876,[3] but at the time of General Sutter's death in 1880, both were married. Anna Eliza became the wife of Howard Hull of Lititz. After his death in 1885, she and her sons, Howard and Richard, moved to Acapulco and lived with her father there. Later she married her cousin Victor Alphonse Link, son of her father's only sister.

The younger girl, María del Carmen, married Jesse Smith of Woonsocket, Rhode Island. She died there of pneumonia in May, 1890.[4]

Nine children were born to Sutter and Nicolasa Solís.

Cristina, the eldest, was born in 1874 and was married on September 3, 1894, to Jan Herman Munch, a professor, who later changed

---

[1] Hull to the writer, Feb. 21, 1941.
[2] Dana, *Sutter*, p. 411; *Sacramento Union*, July 5, 1880.
[3] *Alta Calif.*, Mar. 13, 1876.
[4] *Sacramento Union*, July 5, 1890; Grace H. Hall, Harris Institute Library, Woonsocket, to the writer, Mar. 15, 1941.

his name legally to van Wolbeck. They came to San Francisco in 1920 with their four children. Mrs. van Wolbeck died May 28, 1935.[5]

Carlos Alfredo, born in 1875, was the second child. He died in 1880.[6]

Reginaldo Sutter was born in 1878. In 1914, when relations were tense between the United States and Mexico, his plantation was confiscated and he was forced to flee the country, leaving his wife and their six children behind. Reginaldo came directly to Sacramento, confident of obtaining employment in the city his father founded. City officials attempted to secure his employment at Sutter's Fort, then owned and maintained by the state as a historical museum; apparently they had little success, for a few weeks later Sutter appealed to the city commissioners for funds to enable him to return to Mexico. More than a year afterwards a public subscription among Sacramento businessmen enabled him to return to his family.[7] In 1934 he was living in San Francisco,[8] but he returned again to Acapulco, where he died on December 27, 1941, after a long illness.[9] At one time Reginaldo was mayor of Acapulco. His citizenship was questioned and he renounced the American birthright derived from his father and declared himself a Mexican citizen.[10]

Juan Norbert, born in 1882, went to sea and became an officer in the American merchant marine. In 1922 he was reported to be an invalid in delicate health, but he evidently returned to the sea, for, at the time of his death of pneumonia in New York on March 1, 1937, he was chief officer of the American-Hawaiian steamship *Columbian*. He was survived by three daughters and two sons.[11]

Arturo Sutter, born two years after Juan Norbert, died in 1885.[12]

Anna, or Anita, born on September 18, 1887, spent part of her childhood in Mexico City, where she attended school and lived with her married sister, probably Cristina. When she learned that her father was on his deathbed and asking for her, she was determined,

   [5] "Claim for Expropriation of Property in Mexico," Aug. 19, 1942, in Sutter, Jr., Papers; *Sacramento Bee*, Feb. 15, 1922.
   [6] Smisor to the writer, July 25, 1941.
   [7] *Sacramento Bee*, May 12 and June 9, 1914; Aug. 18, 1915.
   [8] R. Sutter to Mabel R. Gillis, Feb. 17, 1934.
   [9] Smisor to the writer, July 25, 1941; Hudson to the writer, Apr. 21, 1942.
   [10] Statement by Mrs. Young.
   [11] *Sacramento Bee*, Mar. 23, 1937.
   [12] Smisor to the writer, July 25, 1941.

though only ten years old, to hurry home to Acapulco, but her sister dissuaded her from the long journey by mountain trail. She did return later to Acapulco where the manager hired by her mother to handle the family's business affairs also became her tutor. In 1915 she came to San Francisco, where she still lives, although she has since made several visits to Acapulco. She married William B. Young on January 7, 1920. Mrs. Young is the sole surviving child of Sutter, Jr., and the closest living descendant of General John A. Sutter.

Alfredo C., born in 1890, disappeared in youth and was never heard from. It is thought that, like his brother Juan, he went to sea.[13]

The date of Sofía's birth is uncertain, but she was a minor child when Sutter drew up his will and may have followed Reginaldo. She married a man named Sierra. Sofía has been dead for several years.[14]

In his will Sutter stated that there were nine children, of whom six were living. Carlos Alfredo, Arturo, and at least one other child had died before then. Ernestina Sutter Morlett, daughter of Reginaldo, believes that four children, born before Carlos Alfredo, died in infancy.[15]

---

[13] Idem.; *Sacramento Bee,* Mar. 23, 1937.

[14] "Claim for Expropriation of Property in Mexico," Aug. 19, 1942, in Sutter, Jr., Papers.

[15] Smisor to the writer, July 25, 1941.

Appendix II

THE city's title to the property presented by Sutter, Jr., was first tested in 1873 in the precedent-making case of *Mayo* v. *Wood*. On September 5, 1862, the Board of Supervisors of Sacramento City passed an ordinance which gave to the Union Park Association the right to occupy the gift block bounded by B, C, 21st, and 22nd Streets. Here and on adjoining blocks owned by the association a race track was built. The following September, William Mesick deeded this same block, which he had secured in his purchase from Sutter, Jr., to L. H. Foote, who in turn conveyed it on April 17, 1868, to Eli Mayo. The race track at this time was occupied by Robert Allen, who leased it from the association. Mayo, by successful suit, forced the ejection of Allen, then allowed him to remain for the insignificant rental of ten cents! On January 1, 1873, A. A. Wood leased the race track from the State Agricultural Society (which had meanwhile bought the controlling interest in the old association) with the understanding that one block was occupied only by city consent. Mayo promptly brought suit in the Sixth Judicial District Court against Wood, but the judge ruled that Mayo had not shown his right of possession and decided for the defendant. Mayo carried the case to the state Supreme Court, which declared that the block was city property by virtue of Sutter's gift in 1849, that Sutter had no title to give to Mesick in 1855, and that consequently the defendant should be sustained.[1] The

---

[1] *Mayo* v. *Wood*, in *Calif. Reports*, L (1875), 171–176; Calif. Supreme Court, [Cases, old series], No. 4313, in office of Secretary of State of California, Archives.

case thus made the city's ownership quite clear and furnished precedent to several later suits revolving about young Sutter's gift lands.

The next effort to secure a parcel of these lands came in 1893, when John Bidwell, Edgar B. Carroll, a Sacramento resident, and A. C. Hinkson, an attorney, wrote separate letters to Sutter at Acapulco, urging him to assent to use of the popular plaza block bounded by Ninth, Tenth, I, and J Streets as the site for a large new hotel. Such a hotel, it was felt, was necessary in order to keep the capital at Sacramento.[2] Sutter evidently insisted that if the plaza be converted to private use he should receive compensation as for an ordinary sale of property.[3] The deal never went through, the capital remained at Sacramento, and today hundreds of the city's elderly citizens idle under the plaza's wide-armed elm trees.

In 1910, thirteen years after his death, another letter addressed to John A. Sutter, Jr., arrived at Acapulco. In it Hinkson, who had been attorney for the hotel syndicate, declared that one of the gift parks had for some years been leased by the city to persons who had been using it for purely personal ends. Hinkson indicated a willingness to prosecute a suit, *mutually satisfactory and beneficial,* for its recovery.[4] The letter went unanswered, but it sowed the seed for the later action by Sutter's widow.

From August 26, 1872, until June 30, 1924, the block bounded by Fifteenth, Sixteenth, I, and J Streets was used for public school purposes. Then the city proposed to erect an auditorium there with the understanding that when it was not being used for public purposes admission might be charged for plays and other entertainments. A test case against the city was instituted in the Superior Court by H. J. Futterer, a property owner. The California Supreme Court, to which the case was appealed, upheld the action of the city, declaring that the erection of an auditorium, even if admission be charged, came within young Sutter's provision that the block be *for the public use . . . as the future incoperated authoritys of said city from tim[e] to time declare and deturmine.*[5]

---

[2] Bidwell to Sutter, Jr., Apr. 29, 1893, copy in possession of Frank B. Durkee, Sacramento; Hinkson to Sutter, Jr., Jan. 23, 1910, in Sutter, Jr., Papers.

[3] Hinkson to Sutter, Jr., Jan. 23, 1910.

[4] Idem.

[5] *Futterer* v. *City of Sacramento,* in *Calif. Reports,* CXCVI (1925), 248–259; *Pacific Reporter,* CCXXXVII (1925), 48–53.

On January 31, 1924, the city abandoned Seventeenth Street from B to C and the alley between Sixteenth and Eighteenth Streets to allow for the construction of a plant by the California Packing Corporation. This action touched off a suit by the Sutter heirs. Stella E. Gramer, as administratrix of the estate of Sutter, Jr., on August 17, 1926, filed suit in the Sacramento Superior Court against the city, contending that once these streets were closed to public use for the benefit of private interests, they reverted to the heirs. Into the case now stepped Alphonse Sutter, Jr., grandson of General Sutter, who intervened through his attorney, Mrs. Helen Van Gulpen Harris, on May 19, 1927. Alphonse contended that there had been no actual payment of money in the 1848 transfer of land from father to son, and that his uncle, John A. Sutter, Jr., had merely acted as agent for John A. Sutter, Sr., in the disposition of lands in Sacramento. If there was to be any reversion of property to Sutter descendants, he wanted to be sure that it went to those whom he considered the closer heirs of the old pioneer. Alphonse died five months later, but Mrs. Harris carried on for the estate.

Judge W. A. Anderson ruled on November 10, 1930, that neither the plaintiff nor the intervener had any interest in the property. Five months later the case was re-opened, but Judge Anderson dismissed it, whereupon it was appealed on August 12, 1931, to the California Supreme Court. Nearly four years later, on February 19, 1935, the court found for the city, noting that between 1862 and 1921 some thirteen previous ordinances abandoning streets had been passed in Sacramento without complaint.[6]

But Mrs. Harris was not through, and on March 23, 1929, she filed another futile suit against the California Packing Corporation for $25,000 damages involving the same street and alley.[7] And on July 12, 1929, she and Captain Frank Sutter Link, grandson of Sutter, Jr., filed two more damage suits. The first was against the Southern Pacific Co. for $300,000 damages to property on Sixth, Seventh, C, D, E, F, and G Streets, covered by the railroad's extensive shops and yards, and rental of $5,000 a month since August, 1924. The second was against the city and the Pacific Gas & Electric Co. for

[6] *Gramer* v. *City of Sacramento*, Sacramento Superior Court, Dept. No. 3, case No. 36,785, judgment No. 26,276.

[7] *Sacramento Bee*, Mar. 23, 1929.

$10,000 damages to property on T and U Streets and $200 monthly rental since August, 1924.[8]

There was also litigation over the waterfront, which Sutter, Jr., had given to the Front Street property owners pending the incorporation of the city and the selection of proper city authorities. Among the choicest of commercial properties on the river, it was soon taken over by such corporations as the Sacramento Valley Railroad, whose line to Folsom in 1855 was the first railroad in California, the California Steam Navigation Co., which ruled the river trade with an iron grip after its organization in 1854, and the Central Pacific Railroad, which completed the first transcontinental rail line in 1869.

After the Mesick decisions by the state Supreme Court in 1858, Mesick on May 6, 1859, sold for ten dollars to Brannan, Grahame, Gilbert A. Grant, William Harney, and Frederick Werner, the river frontage down to Q Street. On July 5 of the same year the part from I to Q Streets was purchased from them by John H. Brewer for $10,000.[9] It was not until 1868, however, that Brewer sought to eject the transportation companies from the property. The corporations filed answers to Brewer's suit, but for some reason the case was never pressed to a conclusion, and though Brewer lived until 1911 he never again sought possession of the property he allegedly owned.[10]

There was occasional activity from time to time by various claimants, particularly by the city and the Southern Pacific in 1905 and 1906, but it was not until 1915 that the situation really came to a head. In that year four claimants were in court seeking the waterfront property, said at that time to be worth about $3,000,000:

1. Two groups of Front Street property owners claimed, under young Sutter's original deed, all the waterfront except that part used as streets.

2. The city of Sacramento, as intervener, contended that young Sutter's deed dedicated the streets to public use, and that Front Street extended to the low water mark of the river.

3. The Southern Pacific Co., successor to the three transportation companies mentioned above, based its claim on various grants (some without time limits) made by Sacramento city authorities.

---

[8] *Ibid.*, July 13, 1929.

[9] Sacramento County, *Deed Books*, vol. Z, p. 252, 324–325.

[10] *Sacramento Bee*, June 22, 23, 1914; Aug. 28, 1915.

4. The heirs of John H. Brewer contended that their title had passed to them through various sales since young Sutter had first sold to Brannan, Bruce, Grahame, and Wetzlar. They claimed the waterfront from Q Street north to one hundred sixty feet beyond I Street.

On August 4, 1915, the Southern Pacific, in an effort to quiet title, filed suit to bring all claimants into court to settle all questions of waterfront ownership in one case.[11] Individuals were promptly eliminated when Judge W. C. Van Fleet on December 1 dismissed the case of the Front Street property owners, declaring that their only remedy would be a damage suit. The statute of limitations had outlawed such a suit years before. The decision left only the city and the railroad in the field.[12]

For several years the case was bounced about the courts on amended complaints and appeals until April 14, 1919, when the federal court threw it out for lack of prosecution. In 1924 the case was momentarily revived when Councilman C. H. S. Bidwell introduced a successful resolution to inquire into the advisability of the city's reopening the case.[13] It was turned over to the Committee on River and Harbor Improvement, where it died.[14] Persistent Bidwell again brought up the question in 1930; it was turned over to the city attorney, and that officer, Hugh Bradford, compiled and submitted an excellent and comprehensive report on the case.[15] There the matter stands today.

There seems to be little question that the city is the actual owner of the waterfront property. The original deed gave the Front Street lot owners *exclusive use* of the land facing them, all the way to the river, only until the city could be incorporated and municipal authority established. Included in the Bradford report is an opinion rendered by City Attorney Archibald Yell on August 11, 1914, at the request of the Crane Co. This opinion declared that the city had exercised constant control over the waterfront since 1849, when it enforced

[11] *Sacramento Bee,* Aug. 28, 1915.

[12] See Franck R. Havenner, "Burrel G. White Clients Lose Suit for Waterfront," and "City's Claim not Affected by Decision," *Sacramento Bee,* Dec. 1, 2, 1915.

[13] Sacramento City Clerk's office, *Council Minutes,* June 26, 1924, XXXI, 303; *Sacramento Bee,* June 27, 1924.

[14] Sacramento City Clerk's office, *Index of Council Committees.*

[15] Sacramento City Clerk's office, *Report to City Council by Hugh Bradford,* Feb. 27, 1930.

clearance of obstructions from the river bank; that for sixty-five years no person owning lots on Front Street had ever asserted right or title to the waterfront; that the city had never permitted anyone to occupy or have exclusive use of any portion of the street; and that anyone using the land between Front Street and the river always had done so under specific license from the city.

Bibliography

Bibliography

1. Books and Periodicals

The Argonaut. San Francisco, 1877–.

ASSOCIATED PIONEERS OF THE TERRITORIAL DAYS OF CALIFORNIA. *First Annual Meeting and Banquet*. New York, 1875.

BANCROFT, HUBERT HOWE. *History of British Columbia*. San Francisco, 1887.

BANCROFT, HUBERT HOWE. *History of California*. San Francisco, 1884–1890. 7 volumes.

BANCROFT, HUBERT HOWE. *History of Mexico*. San Francisco, 1882–1888. 6 volumes.

BANCROFT, HUBERT HOWE. *Popular Tribunals*. San Francisco, 1887. 2 volumes.

BEALS, CARLETON. *Porfirio Díaz, Dictator of Mexico*. Philadelphia, J. B. Lippincott, 1932.

BLACK, SAMUEL T. *San Diego County, California; a Record of Settlement, Organization, Progress and Achievement*. Chicago, S. J. Clarke Publishing Co., 1913. 2 volumes.

BOGGS, MAE HELENE BACON. *My Playhouse Was a Concord Coach, an Anthology of Newspaper Clippings and Documents Relating to Those Who Made California History During the Years 1822–1888*. [Oakland, Printed at the Howell-North Press, 1942].

BRYANT, EDWIN. *What I Saw in California: Being the Journal of a Tour . . . in the Years, 1846–1847*. 7th edition. New York, D. Appleton & Co., 1849.

BURNETT, PETER HARDEMAN. *Recollections and Opinions of an Old Pioneer*. New York, 1880.

California Blue Book. Sacramento, State Printing Office, 1911.

California Historical Society Quarterly. San Francisco, 1922–.

California Reports. Volumes VI (1856), X (1858), L (1875), CXCVI (1925). San Francisco, Sacramento, 1858–1926.

[CHAMBERLAIN, WILLIAM HENRY]. *History of Yuba County, California*. Oakland, Thompson & West, 1879.

COFFIN, GEORGE. *A Pioneer Voyage to California and Round the World, 1849 to 1852, Ship Alhambra*. [Chicago? 1908].

COLTON, WALTER. *Three Years in California [1846–1849]*. New York, Cincinnati, 1850.

COLVILLE, SAMUEL. *The Sacramento Directory for the Year 1853–54 . . . Together with a History of Sacramento Written by Dr. John F. Morse*. Sacramento, 1853.

Commercial Relations of the United States with Foreign Countries, 1873, 1875, 1876, 1884–1885, 1886–1887. Washington, 1874, 1876, 1877, 1886, 1888.

CREELMAN, JAMES. *Díaz, Master of Mexico*. New York, D. Appleton & Co., 1912.

CROSS, IRA B. *Financing an Empire; History of Banking in California*. Chicago, San Francisco, S. J. Clarke Publishing Co., 1927. 4 volumes.

CULVER, J. HORACE. *The Sacramento City Directory. January 1, 1851*. Sacramento, 1851.

DANA, JULIAN. *Sutter of California, a Biography*. New York, Press of the Pioneers, 1934.

DAVIS, WILLIAM HEATH. *Sixty Years in California*. San Francisco, 1889.

DAVIS, WINFIELD J. *An Illustrated History of Sacramento County, California*. Chicago, 1890.

Dictionary of American Biography. New York, Charles Scribner's Sons, 1928–1937. 21 volumes.

Directory of the County of Placer, for the Year 1861. Compiled by R. J. Steele, James P. Bull, and F. I. Houston. San Francisco, 1861.

Engineerogram. Sacramento, American Society of Civil Engineers, Sacramento Section, 1939–.

FOSTER, JOHN W. *Diplomatic Memoirs*. Boston, Houghton Mifflin Co., 1909. 2 volumes.

GREENE, LAURENCE. *The Filibuster*. Indianapolis, Bobbs-Merrill, 1937.

Grizzly Bear Magazine. Los Angeles, 1907–.

GUDDE, ERWIN G. *Sutter's Own Story; the Life of General John Au-*

gustus Sutter and the History of New Helvetia in the Sacramento Valley. New York, G. P. Putnam's Sons, 1936.

HISTORICAL RECORDS SURVEY, CALIFORNIA. *Calendar of the Major Jacob Rink Snyder Collection of the Society of California Pioneers.* San Francisco, Northern California Historical Records Survey Project, 1940.

Hutchings' Illustrated California Magazine. San Francisco, 1856–1861.

KIMBALL, CHARLES P. *The San Francisco City Directory, September 1, 1850.* San Francisco, 1850.

LABATT, HENRY J. *Reports of Cases Determined in the District Courts of the State of California.* San Francisco, 1858. 2 volumes.

LIENHARD, HEINRICH. *Californien Unmittelbar vor und nach der Entdeckung des Goldes.* Zurich, 1898.

LIENHARD, HEINRICH. *A Pioneer at Sutter's Fort, 1846–1850, the Adventures of Heinrich Lienhard ... Translated, Edited, and Annotated by Marguerite Eyer Wilbur from the Original German Manuscript.* Los Angeles, Calafía Society, 1941.

MORGAN, A. W. & Co. *San Francisco City Directory, September, 1852.* San Francisco, 1852.

MORSE, JOHN F., *see* Colville, Samuel. *The Sacramento Directory for the Year 1853–54.*

New Helvetia Diary; a Record of Events Kept by John A. Sutter and His Clerks at New Helvetia, California, from September 9, 1845, to May 25, 1848. San Francisco, Grabhorn Press in Arrangement with the Society of California Pioneers, 1939.

Official Register of the United States, 1883, 1887. Washington, 1884, 1887.

Oregon Historical Quarterly. Portland, Oregon Historical Society, 1900–.

Overland Monthly. San Francisco, 1868–1875, 1880–1935.

PARKER, JAMES M. *The San Francisco Directory for the Year 1852–53.* San Francisco, 1852.

PARKES, HENRY BAMFORD. *History of Mexico.* Boston, Houghton Mifflin Co., 1938.

PLUMBE, JOHN. *A Faithful Translation of the Papers Respecting the Grant Made by Governor Alvarado to John A. Sutter. Reprinted from the Original Pamphlet Published in 1850 by John Plumbe, with an Introduction by Neal Harlow.* Sacramento, Sacramento Book Collectors Club, 1942.

POWELL, LAWRENCE CLARK. *Philosopher Pickett, the Life and Writings of Charles Edward Pickett, Esq., of Virginia.* Berkeley and Los Angeles, University of California Press, 1942.

PRIESTLEY, HERBERT INGRAM. *The Mexican Nation, a History.* New York, Macmillan Co., 1923.

PROSCH, THOMAS WICKHAM. *McCarver and Tacoma.* Seattle, Lowman & Hanford [1906].

RAMEY, EARL. *The Beginnings of Marysville.* San Francisco, California Historical Society, 1936.

REED, G. WALTER. *History of Sacramento County, California.* Los Angeles, Historic Record Co., 1923.

ROLPH, GEORGE M. *Something about Sugar, its History, Growth, Manufacture and Distribution.* San Francisco, J. J. Newbegin, 1917.

SACRAMENTO BEE. *Sacramento Guide Book.* Sacramento, 1939.

SCHLIEMANN, HEINRICH. *Schliemann's First Visit to America, 1850–1851; Edited by Shirley H. Weber.* Cambridge, Mass., Harvard University Press, 1942.

SHUCK, OSCAR T. *Representative and Leading Men of the Pacific.* San Francisco, 1870.

SIOLI, PAOLO, PUBLISHER. *Historical Souvenir of Eldorado County, California.* Oakland, 1883.

SOCIETY OF CALIFORNIA PIONEERS. *Quarterly.* San Francisco, 1924–.

SWASEY, WILLIAM F. *The Early Days and Men of California.* Oakland [1891].

TAYLOR, BAYARD. *Eldorado, or, Adventures in the Path of Empire.* New York, 1850. 2 volumes.

Themis. Sacramento, 1889–1894.

THOMPSON AND WEST, PUBLISHERS. *History of Sacramento County, California.* Oakland, 1880.

U. S. v. Sutter, *Supreme Court of the United States. No. 258. The United States, Appellants, vs. John A. Sutter. Appeal from the District Court, U. S., for the Northern District of California.* [n.p., 1863].

ZOLLINGER, JAMES PETER. *Sutter, the Man and His Empire.* New York, Oxford University Press, 1939.

II. MANUSCRIPTS

BIDWELL COLLECTION. (California State Library.)

CALIFORNIA SUPREME COURT. [Cases, Old Series] No. 4313. (Secretary of State of California, Archives.)

LARKIN, THOMAS OLIVER. *Documents for the History of California, 1839–1856.* (Bancroft Library.)

LIENHARD, HEINRICH. *Memoiren.* (In the possession of Mrs. E. J. Magnuson, Minneapolis, Minnesota.)

McCHRISTIAN, PATRICK. *Narrative, as Given by Him to Robert A. Thompson, Editor of the Sonoma Democrat, November 1, 1855.* (Bancroft Library.)

PIONEER FILE. (California State Library.)

SACRAMENTO CITY CLERK'S OFFICE. *Council Minutes.*

SACRAMENTO CITY CLERK'S OFFICE. *Index of Council Committees.*

SACRAMENTO CITY CLERK'S OFFICE. *Report to City Council by Hugh Bradford.* February 27, 1930.

SACRAMENTO COUNTY RECORDER'S OFFICE. *Deed Books.*

SACRAMENTO COUNTY RECORDER'S OFFICE. *Powers of Attorney.*

SIXTH JUDICIAL COURT (Sacramento). *Cases.*

SUTTER COLLECTION. (California State Library.)

SUTTER, JR., COLLECTION. (California State Library.)

SUTTER, JR., PAPERS. (In possession of Mrs. Anna Sutter Young, San Francisco. Copies of many in Sutter, Jr., Collection, California State Library.)

U. S. STATE DEPARTMENT. *Appointment Papers.* (National Archives. Microfilm copies of some pertinent documents in the California State Library.)

U. S. STATE DEPARTMENT. *Consular Correspondence, Despatches, Acapulco.* (National Archives. Microfilm copies of some pertinent documents in the California State Library.)

VALLEJO, MARIANO GUADALUPE. *Documentos para la Historia de California, 1769–1850.* (Bancroft Library.)

III. NEWSPAPERS

Alta California. San Francisco, 1849–1891.
California Chronicle (daily). San Francisco, 1853–1858.
California Star and Californian. San Francisco, 1848.
Californian. Monterey and San Francisco, 1846–1848.
Daily Evening Post. San Francisco, 1871–1913.
Daily Herald. San Francisco, 1850–1862.
Democratic State Journal. Sacramento, 1852–1858.
New York Herald. New York, 1835–1924.
Pioneer. San Jose, 1877–1883, 1893–1901.
Placer Times. Sacramento, 1849–1851.
Sacramento Bee. Sacramento, 1857–.
Sacramento Transcript. Sacramento, 1850–1851.
Sacramento Union. Sacramento, 1851–.
San Francisco Call. San Francisco, 1856–.
San Francisco Chronicle. San Francisco, 1865–.
San Francisco Examiner. San Francisco, 1865–.

Index

Index